Ruth Carter Stapleton

Brother Billy

Harper & Row, Publishers

New York, Hagerstown
San Francisco, London

Portions of this work originally appeared in *Woman's Day*.

Photo of Mr. Earl Carter courtesy of Wide World.

FIRST EDITION
Designed by Janice Stern

Library of Congress Cataloging in Publication Data

Stapleton, Ruth Carter.
  Brother Billy.
    1. Carter, Billy. 2. Presidents—United States—Brothers and sisters—Biography.
3. Carter, Jimmy, 1924– I. Title. E874.C29S72 1978   975.8'913 [B]   78–2173
ISBN 0–06–014063–1

78 79 80 81 82 10 9 8 7 6 5 4 3 2

To the hero of my brother
Billy's life: Daddy

Contents

Photo section follows page 150.

Abraham Lincoln said: "God
must love the common people.
He made so many of them."

Part I

Growing Up in Plains

It was two days after the presidential inauguration. The crowds in Washington were thinning some, but the festivities were still going on in scattered areas throughout the city. The last social event before my husband and I returned to North Carolina was a reception at the Mexican Embassy for Señora de Lopez Portillo, wife of the president of Mexico.

We were ushered through the embassy entrance and up to the second-floor reception room where a steadily growing crowd was gathering. Television camera lights were focused on the doorway, and the press photographers' flashbulbs punctuated the hall with brilliance each time a new guest arrived. After being introduced to the guest of honor, Señora Portillo, I walked over to the side of the reception room so I could have a better view of the guests as they arrived and enjoy a moment of quiet before the luncheon. A few minutes later, my attention was turned to the doorway by the clicking cameras and blazing strobe lights. I looked around to see who the new arrival could be. "Mr. Henry Kissinger," someone announced. I watched him move around the room with an entourage of cameramen and reporters greeting each guest.

He came slowly in my direction, and then this eminent world figure was standing before me, smiling. Our host turned to him and said, "Mr. Kissinger, I'd like you to meet Mrs. Ruth Stapleton, sister of the President."

"Mrs. Stapleton," Mr. Kissinger said, "it is my pleasure. I'm happy to meet you. May I ask you something personal?"

"Of course," I answered. In the pause before I heard his question, I asked myself what this former Secretary of State, this architect of shuttle diplomacy, this Olympian world diplomat would want to ask me.

"Would you please tell me about your brother Billy?"

Billy! He wanted to know about my brother Billy!

As I later reflected on his question, I realized he was asking something which has been on the minds of millions of Americans. Who is this now-famous gas-pumping, pub-operating peanut man from Plains? What is Billy Carter really like?

1

A New Arrival

It is generally known that Earl and Lillian Carter had two sons. Jimmy, the older, grew up to be a politician. Billy, the younger, became a famous peanut merchant, a popular host at Carter's Georgia Amoco Station in Plains, a much-sought-after celebrity whose well-paid public appearances range from tossing out the first ball at an Oakland ball game to sharing his homespun humor on national TV. His name has become a household word, and—it was almost inevitable—a beer was named after him. His brother has learned to live in the shadow of Billy's incredible national fame and popularity with noteworthy humility and grace.

Billy's story began on March 29, 1937, in a small, sleepy, anonymous, now suddenly world-famous village of Plains. William Alton Carter was the fourth child of the Carter household. A brother and two sisters preceded him: James Earl on October 1, 1924; Gloria on October 22, 1926; and I, Ruth, on August 7, 1929. Billy was later to say, "I have a brother who wants to be President, one sister who rides motorcycles, and another who is a holy-roller preacher. That makes me the only sane one in the family." The fact is that Jimmy did become President of the United States. Gloria does ride motorcycles on frequent occasions with her husband, Walter. And I do speak to religious and secular organizations about the power of the love of God to heal the mind and body. But I will abstain from any judgment on our relative sanity.

Both Gloria and I were in grammar school when we learned that we were going to have a new baby brother or sister. I remember it was a hot August day when we were given the good news. We were living on our farm outside of Plains. Mother told Gloria while I was out of the house, spending the afternoon in town with Rosalynn Smith, my best friend and Jimmy's future wife. When I returned and began to climb the steps into the large screen porch of our home, Gloria came up to me and asked, "Have you heard about Mother?" The look on her face, the tone of her voice told me it was something exciting. But she was acting very calm and cool about it. "No, tell me."

"She's going to have a baby."

"Oh, Gloria!" And we embraced.

During the months of my mother's pregnancy, her weight ballooned sixty pounds. She blamed her overweight on her passion for hickory nuts. Her maid, Annie Mae Hollis, brought her a box of nuts every afternoon. Mother would lie in bed and read, her favorite pastime, while consuming her daily ration of nuts. She wasn't too concerned about the extra weight, but five weeks before Billy's birth, Mother was walking by Lady, our Shetland pony. It kicked her, knocking her on her back. As she fell her tailbone struck a concrete grease trap. Dr. Sam Wise, her physician, ordered her to remain in bed. What he didn't tell her was that his forty-year-old patient had a serious heart murmur.

The late-in-life pregnancy was difficult for Mother, but Daddy was thrilled. In fact, he wanted twins. He had always wanted twins, but his babies never came in pairs. Businessman that he was, he thought a little incentive would help Mother produce those twins. He saw her size as a promising sign that they were on the way, so he told her that if she gave him the desired duo he would give her a love gift of one thousand dollars.

She felt the first contractions on the afternoon of Easter Sunday. Aunt Elizabeth Braunstein, Mother's sister and a registered nurse like Mother, was caring for her. She called out to Daddy, who was standing by the woodpile talking to his three children. "Earl," she said, "Lillian has begun labor."

A look of anxiety came over Daddy's face. He had been very worried about Mother's heart condition. There was much concern that she would not be able to endure the strain of the delivery. He turned and ran through the back door into the house. He went to Mother's side and said, "Darlin', we'll get you to the hospital right away." Mother's mother, Mary Ida Gordy, who had come from Richland, Georgia, to be near her daughter, spoke pleasantly about the blessed event, masking her fears.

As they departed for the hospital, Mother came up to each of her children and kissed us good-bye. Then Daddy eased her into the front seat of our green 1937 Oldsmobile, ran around to the driver's side, and began his anxious race to Plains Hospital.

When they arrived, Daddy refused to leave his wife's side. Dr. Sam arrived soon after. Daddy scrutinized his every expression to see if he could detect signs of concern, but Dr. Sam kept a poker face as he went through a routine he knew perfectly after the experience of delivering several hundred other babies. As the hours wore on, Daddy grew more worried about Mother and his unborn son, daughter, or twins. By now he didn't care. He just wanted his wife and their new baby alive and well. He would give everything he owned in the world to assure that, but he couldn't negotiate a deal. He just waited and prayed.

In the wee hours of the morning after Easter Sunday, Billy was born. He had obviously enjoyed the daily hickory nut binge as much as Mother. He was a nine-pound butterball. Daddy didn't want to leave his new son's side, and Mother refused to let them take him to the nursery. She didn't want him out of her sight either.

The postscript to this episode is that Mother refused to concede that there wasn't another baby in her womb. She kept trying to have that second child, Billy's twin, but after over an hour she realized that God had not cooperated. The disappointment was minor. Daddy gave her the one thousand dollars anyway. Billy was such a treasure she didn't really mind. Nor did Daddy.

When the tiny new Carter returned home with Mother a week later, he was met by the whole family, all eager to spoil this baby rotten. And we did.

The house to which Billy came was a large, comfortable wood-frame structure with a lawn stretching between the front screen porch and the red dirt country road that ran from Plains to nowhere, as my childhood memory recalls.

The main entrance to the house led through the enclosed porch into a spacious living room, and the furniture there was part of the Carter family. To the right of the front door against the wall was a black-stained hardwood desk with two pigeon-hole shelves on its high back. When Jimmy recently discovered it all dust-covered in a storage room, he said, "Oh, hello, Mother." We knew what he meant. Mother always left a note sticking out of the top right pigeonhole if she was not to be home when we arrived on the bus after school. One of those unexplainable repeated traumas of my early childhood always occurred when I walked in the front door as a first grader and saw a note from Mother in the desk. I would fall to the floor of the living room and cry uncontrollably because Mother wasn't there and I feared she would never come back.

Other memories are attached to the furniture of the living room. Against the front wall was an upright Baldwin piano where we struggled with lessons and delighted in songfests or just played our teen-age favorites with a friend. Against the left wall was Daddy's big brown leather easy chair, and to the right of that was our old three-foot-tall, curved-top radio. The most memorable thing about the radio was sitting with the whole family each Sunday evening and listening to "The Jack Benny Hour" with its opening signature song, "J-E-L-L-O."

To the right of the living room was the bedroom shared by Gloria and me. Running from the living room to the back of the house was a wide hallway. The first room to the left past the living room was the dining room, and across the hall from it was Mother and Daddy's bedroom. Every room had a fireplace, our only source of heat in the fall and winter chill. But these two rooms had a fire in the fireplace every day, morning and night, when the weather was cool. The large, heavy walnut table in the dining room was the study center for the children. While school was in session, each night would find us seated around the table with our books and papers stacked on it, reading or writing by the light of kerosene lamps, since we had no electricity until I was almost nine years old.

On each side of the fireplace was a tiny anteroom. The one on the left served as the family library. It contained scores of volumes of everything from Tarzan and Mark Twain's writings to Emily Dickinson, George Eliot, and Chaucer. I remember, too, the dog-eared copy of Dickens's *A Christmas Carol,* which we so often read during the holy season.

The other anteroom was filled with games. The Carters were all competitive. By the age of ten, the children learned to play bridge. On almost any given night, one could find us locked in a furious struggle to win some game. Usually it was a fight over Boardwalk, Park Place, or the Reading Railroad in our favorite game, Monopoly. Daddy was the patriarch, but he was never spared the humbling experience of defeat if we could win against him. Scrabble and Parcheesi were also very popular. At five, I didn't win much, but I tried. No one hated to lose more than Jimmy. If, as tradition says, English battles were won on the playing fields of Eton, I wonder if the White House was won in a dining room in Plains. The will to win certainly was honed, if not forged, there.

The next room down the hall adjoining the dining room was the breakfast room where we always ate our meals when we had no guests. At suppertime all the Carter children brought a book to the table to read. It was quite normal to prop a book up against a sugar bowl or drinking glass and devour it with a meal. This habit was later to create a crisis in Billy's marriage, but in our home it was accepted routine.

Behind the breakfast room at the back of the house was a large kitchen, and across the hall was Jimmy's bedroom. We learned early that if we were involved in any noisy horseplay, it must never be around his bedroom. Jimmy was a happy but serious young man, with more of both qualities than any of his teen-ager friends, and when he was home he was usually reading or studying. On his bedroom mantel was a three-foot-long, finely detailed three-masted sailing vessel my mother's brother, Uncle Tom Gordy, who was a sailor, had given him. It was more than a boat to Jimmy. It was part of a dream that was fulfilled when he went to the United States Naval Academy.

The day Billy was brought home he was carried to a crib in

my parents' bedroom. He shared the room with them until Jimmy went off to college three years later, when the back bedroom then became Billy's until the family moved from the farm into Plains seven years later.

2

Roots

The Carters were relatively new to Plains, but their roots went deep into the soil of America. The first Carter to immigrate to America was Thomas, who came from England in 1635 as an indentured servant. After working for six years to purchase his freedom, he became a soldier of fortune. Then, in 1659, he settled down and became a successful farmer and respected leader in Isle Wight County, Virginia.

Thomas's descendants continued his restless ways. Each succeeding generation traveled to new regions, from Virginia to Bertie County, North Carolina, then down to McDuffe, Georgia. Each move was marked by success and social involvement. But as in every family, there were also tragedies. The violent death of our great-grandfather, Walker Carter, began a part of the family folklore that was to be told for generations to come.

Walker, who was born in 1832, fought in the Civil War and returned home safely only to be tragically knifed to death in 1873 in a dispute with his business partner. His wife, Mary Ann, died of grief within hours of his death. Among the four orphaned children left was William, our grandfather and Billy's namesake. He was only fifteen at the time of his father's death. He grew up to own three sawmills and rent out a store. But when he was forty-five years of age, like his father, he too was murdered while trying to retrieve a desk he owned from a man who rented his store.

In 1904, a year after William's death, his wife, Nina, moved her family of five, including our father, James Earl, who was then six years old, to the little rural community of Plains of Dura. That name was later shortened to Plains—Plains, Georgia.

Plains was a quiet, sleepy place. Everyone knew each other and every person always seemed to have a mental record of what everyone else was doing. A secret was rare. The town's open-book life led to an accepted greeting and inquiry like, "Good morning, heard you went to Americus yesterday," or "Hello, how's your mother since she moved to Albany?"

The few stores in Plains cozied up to one another in a single block, with an overhang which covered the sidewalk, bordered by a hitching rail. When I was growing up, there was a post office, a drugstore, a grocery, and Uncle Buddy Carter's Plains Mercantile. At the back of his store was a tall counter which was the town bank. On the first floor one could buy farm tools, household items, ready-to-wear clothes, groceries, Christmas toys, and a whole catalog of necessary and unnecessary things. Upstairs, there was even more. The barber set up shop in town once a week. The men of Plains had little need for one because the man of the house usually had the job of trimming the shaggy heads of both boys and girls.

Few families ever moved away. New families seldom moved into town. Plains was Plains was Plains. For around fifty years no new houses were even built. Time didn't stand still in our hometown, but it seemed to have moved more slowly than in most places in our country.

As the Carter family became established in Plains and the

children began to grow up, Uncle Buddy, Daddy's older brother, assumed the role of surrogate father. He was a good and gentle man with a strong streak of racial bigotry. His mores were strictly Bible Belt—no smoking, no drinking, no swearing. He even frowned on slang. But these characteristics didn't lessen his ability to give Daddy the affection he needed.

Daddy had immense energy and drive. As soon as he was old enough to count and wait on customers, he went to work in Uncle Buddy's store. He continued to work there as a young man for one hundred dollars a month. But at seventeen, tired of his routine in Plains, he left and went to Texas where he worked as a cowboy for two years. That adventure convinced him that Plains was home. He returned and sank his meager savings into an ice house. Then he opened a laundry and cleaning establishment called The Pressing Club. He soon proved himself to be the best businessman in Plains.

"Everything Earl touched turned to gold," Uncle Buddy observed years later. He was right; Daddy did have a Midas touch. Uncle Buddy often told how Daddy, even as a little boy, had a talent for making money. When he was only ten years old he collected scrap iron and sold it. "He was a hustler and enjoyed working hard."

As Daddy grew older he felt hemmed in by some of his older brother's prohibitions. He was always a temperate man, but he enjoyed a drink with a couple of Camel cigarettes each evening. All his life he kept his emotional distance from those who insisted that abstinence was next to Godliness, and in Deep South Baptist territory that included quite a few people.

Daddy's faith in Christ was real but not vocal. At one time he taught Sunday School and was secretary of the church board, but later gave it up. Like Billy today, he was suspicious of the pious who refuse to observe those common good things like honesty in business and charity where it was needed.

Though Daddy would not join the Ku Klux Klan, he was a son of the Old South. He refused even to discuss the idea of integration. Years later this was one of the few subjects that Jimmy, after returning from Annapolis, ever argued about with his father. Mother was the one who, as a nurse, saw that blacks and whites were equal in birth and death and should share equality in life between those two points.

Daddy was a paradox in many ways. He had a profound love and respect for people. And he didn't resist change where he saw its value. Taking a cue from his father-in-law, Jim Jack Gordy, he was an early supporter of rural free delivery, which did for rural postal service what the Rural Electrification Administration did for providing electricity to the rural regions of our country. In Daddy's day, RFD was considered by many a radical, socialist, Robin Hood scheme which robbed the rich to give to the poor. Daddy knew better. The poor and the not so poor needed postal service as much as he did, even if he would carry more of the tax load. He wasn't dragged screaming and kicking into the twentieth century. Had he lived to see his son elected President, he would have proudly applauded Jimmy's stand on civil rights in our country and human rights in every nation of the world.

Nineteen miles west of Plains is the town of Richland, Georgia, population: 5,243. This is where Lillian Gordy was born and lived until the age of twenty-one, when she came to the school of nursing at the Plains Hospital. Her father, Jim Jack Gordy, or "Papa," as we called him, was a restless spirit. He was an avid reader and a serious student of history, philosophy, and politics. All his interests were pursued with intensity. He was a U.S. Deputy Marshal in Columbus, Georgia, and then a revenue agent. But he was never really happy until he was appointed postmaster of Richland, the only livelihood he thoroughly enjoyed. That may have been because his first love

beyond his family was politics, and at that time, more than
today, the two were closely connected.

Jim Jack was an exceptionally handsome man. He had dark
hair and a full mustache under an aquiline nose. His deep-set
eyes were dark and intense, his body lean and muscular, and he
was the frequent object of pursuit by young ladies who wanted
to meet him at the altar. Finally, a young beauty named Claudine Phillips mesmerized him with her charm. He proposed to
her and she accepted. But on the day of the wedding, he realized
his mistake and could not face Claudine. He packed up what
belongings he could and fled to Texas. After ten months of
exile, he returned home only to be conquered by a petite young
lady named Mary Ida Nicholson. She became the consuming
love of his life.

Mary Ida knew her man. When Jim Jack proposed to her,
she accepted with this proviso: "Jim Jack," she declared, "if
you decide to go through with our wedding, you come by here
an hour early on the wedding day and pick me up. I won't begin
to put on my bridal dress until you arrive. And you will escort
me to the church." He arrived on time, drove her in a carriage
to the church, and that day she became Mary Ida Gordy.

This high-spirited lady understood her mercurial, unpredict-
able, intense husband. Mary Ida adjusted with little comment
and no anger to Jim Jack's many job changes. She knew he was
a big man who felt confined. Then he became postmaster of
Richland and made his mark. He conceived of the idea of rural
free delivery. He kept explaining and advocating this innovation to his close friend, Congressman Tom Watson of Georgia,
who, once convinced, implemented the idea through federal
legislation. Jim Jack gained the deserved reputation of being the
most politically knowledgeable man in Webster and Stewart
counties. As evidence of his abilities, he retained his appointment as postmaster under four presidential administrations.

The appointment was political and Jim Jack was Republican. It was not until the Roosevelt administration and the advent of civil service that he lost the position. It was a blow, but he adjusted. When he found no other way to be where the political action was, he took the job of custodian at the state capitol building in Atlanta. His daughter, Lillian, fell heir to Jim Jack's enthusiasm. And when she moved to Plains to take up nurse's training, she brought with her the will to have as her husband a man who cared about his community and the workings of government.

The day Lillian Gordy met Earl Carter, she sensed he was the man she had been looking for. He was ambitious, smart, and very handsome. But there was more to him than that. Earl began to court her with the thoroughness he showed in business: flowers, notes, constant attention with cautious but warm displays of affection. His words were usually few, but he expressed deep sensitivity and wisdom. There are few things this man cannot do, she thought, if he really wants to do them.

When Mary Ida Gordy learned that her daughter was to marry Earl Carter, she took her into the bedroom to share some maternal wisdom. "Lillian," she began, "I've raised nine children and a husband. It's not always easy. There will be days when Earl will come home tired and upset and take it out on you. You must be calm and understanding. When the children get cross and the world is upside down, you'll want to give it all up.

"So, Lillian," her mother continued, "my best advice to you is to begin your marriage the first week as I did to prevent storing up all kinds of angers. Every Tuesday since the day Jim Jack and I married, I picked an hour when I could be alone. I would walk out in the yard, down the road, and out into the middle of the large field where I was out of earshot. I would stand there, take a deep breath, and three times scream out as

loud as I could, 'Damn, damn, damn.' Then I would be re-
lieved. The pressure was gone. I'd be able to go back to the
house to take on the responsibilities and pressure without lash-
ing out at your father or giving up. You learn to do something
like this, too."

Lillian never used that particular method, but she did retain
her mother's wisdom: Don't take your frustration out on your
husband.

3

Life on
the Farm

Mother wanted to get married to Daddy right after their engagement. But practical-minded Earl felt it would be wiser to wait until after she completed her nursing intern work at Grady Hospital in Atlanta. Mother reluctantly agreed. Three months later, on September 27, 1923, graduate nurse Lillian Gordy and Earl Carter stood before the Baptist preacher in the parsonage in Plains and were pronounced husband and wife.

The newlyweds rented two rooms on the upper floor of widow Bessie Wellon's big home. Daddy continued to work for Uncle Buddy at the Plains Mercantile and operate the Pressing Club, the laundry business he had purchased a year before their marriage. At that same time he had bought seven hundred acres of farmland. The farm was a business venture. He never intended to put his hand to a plow. His place was behind a desk as an entrepreneur of a growing enterprise. In their second year of marriage he decided that he was ready to expand his business world further. He left Uncle Buddy's Mercantile and with the financial backing of Edgar Shipp, a well-to-do friend, he bought the merchandise appliances from a grocer who had gone out of business in Americus and set up a grocery store in a vacant corner building on the one block of buildings that was downtown Plains. Soon after the grocery store was operating he started a cafe and hired old Mr. Kennedy to run it. All of these investments put Daddy heavily in debt. But he had a boundless faith in the soundness of his purchases and his ability, with a little time and a lot of work, to make them pay off handsomely.

During all this time Mother was working as a nurse in Plains Hospital until she became pregnant with their first child. On October 1, 1924, their son, James Earl Carter, Jr., was born in Plains Hospital. It would be noted years later that he was the first President of the United States to be born in a hospital. Two years later their first daughter, Gloria, was born. Daddy decided his growing family needed a home rather than the small apartment he had been renting in town. So they moved out to the old house on the piece of farmland he owned near Archery, a Seaboard Railroad maintenance station, three miles away from Plains.

On moving day, they arrived at the farm with a Model-T truck laden with furniture and belongings only to find that the people who had vacated the house locked the front and back doors before leaving. Daddy had no key. So he boosted four-year-old Jimmy through a window he was able to pry open, and Jimmy ran around to the front door and let the family in. That was the last time the house was locked as long as the Carter family lived there.

I was born in the house on our farm. On August 7, 1929, in the bed which would be mine for the next seventeen years, Mother brought me into the rural world of southwest Georgia in which I grew up and that, to this day, I especially love.

My earliest memories are of the busy, usually happy days on the farm. Annie Mae Hollis spent much of her day caring for me, curling my long flaxen blond hair and taking me on rides in a small horse carriage pulled by our pony, Lady. I remember tenants cutting wood, cleaning and cooking in the house, and the washerwoman two miles down the road who laundered and folded all of our clothes at her own little house for fifty cents a week.

As the days grew warm we flew kites with long tails made of Daddy's old ties. We made aerial spinners of corncobs and roostertail feathers, and we rolled our barrel hoops down the red clay roads. Many of our most delight-filled days were spent at Magnolia Springs, four miles northeast of Plains. There, in a heavy grove of magnolia trees, was a large pool fed by an artesian spring. The water fountained up from a stone gazebo-like structure and flowed into the concrete-lined pool. A large wooden pavilion stood at one side with a roofed porch extending from it to the water's edge. All of the Carter children learned to dance there to the records found in the pavilion jukebox of such popular musicians as Glenn Miller, the Ink Spots, and Tommy Dorsey. On almost any given Sunday during the warm weather, parents and grandparents would come to relax and chat on the porch while their children swam, danced, and played.

Farmers finished their first plowing in the late spring. Mule-drawn harrows driven by field-wise black tenant farmers broke the soil under the last year's cotton stalks. Laborers followed, dragging the rooted-up stalks and clumps of Bermuda grass to the edge of the fields where they were set afire. When the soil had been cleared off, turning plows dug deep into the damp reddish earth curling it over in long, even furrows. Each furrow was fertilized with an inch width of coarsely ground guano, and in early March corn was planted. As spring warmed the fallow ground, cotton and other crops were put in. The major crop of the area was peanuts.

Before the first peanut plants pushed their tender sprouts

through the soil, the tenant farmers worked from dawn to dark fighting back the tenacious Bermuda grass with long-handled grub hoes. Not until early June when the corn stood to a man's shoulder did there come a two-week "lay-by," a time for rest and recreation. When they returned to the fields, it was to scythe the ripened grain. Then they picked watermelons and hauled them to the railroad cars on the siding at Archery. Next they harvested the cotton, binding it for shipment in huge bales. Finally, everyone pulled peanut vines, deftly jerking them from the red soil, exposing in each clump of roots thirty to fifty plump nuts. The vines were piled like haystacks in the fields so that the nuts could dry in the hot summer sun.

At the age of six each of the three Carter children was given the job of selling peanuts in town. When Gloria became six, eight-year-old Jimmy graduated to the other farm work, and then I reluctantly took over as goober street vendor. Each Saturday morning before sunrise we went out to the nearest field with two large buckets. After filling them with choice peanuts, we then washed them, boiled them in salty water and then packed them in small sacks. Although Daddy instructed her not to, Mother, without letting him know, always helped us prepare the peanuts before she left for her day of nursing duties. With the sacks in a large wicker picnic basket (when Jimmy had the job, he carried two baskets) we hiked along the railroad track about three miles to Plains with our load. I always tried to catch a ride with Daddy.

The crowd in town, which averaged three to four hundred people on a Saturday, milled around, small-talked, and played checkers. We sold our nickel bags of boiled peanuts as we circulated through the clusters of people. Jimmy rather enjoyed the work. He said he knew who the good and bad people of Plains were when he offered his merchandise to them: The good people were the ones who bought his peanuts and the bad people were the ones who wouldn't. Gloria didn't much like the job, but she seldom complained. I passionately disliked it and let Daddy know it. He tended to pamper me, and after two years I happily retired as a peanut vendor although there was no one to replace me. Billy wouldn't come along for eight more years.

Whenever Jimmy accumulated enough money working on the farm to buy some land, Daddy would find a small piece of property his son could buy. It was usually a humble investment at best, but it challenged him to work harder and accumulate more real estate.

As Jimmy approached his teen years, he and Daddy developed a close relationship. They spent many hours together walking through the fields, inspecting one of our many farms, hunting quail, or walking the dogs. The fall of the year was always a special time for father and son. Night after night one could find them sitting in front of the the living room fireplace preparing their guns before the opening day of dove season. It was fascinating to watch them take the guns apart, place them neatly on the floor, then proceed to clean, oil, clean some more, and polish until the shotguns, now reassembled, sparkled like new.

I envied my brother on the morning of the hunt. There was a quiet excitement as he and Daddy checked all their gear, loaded it in pickups, and then drove off to the fields. I knew it wasn't a thing women did, but I so wanted to go with them. My reward came at the end of the day. Daddy always returned home happy and exhausted, and sitting back in his big leather chair, he asked me to take off his boots. On my knees in front of him, I unlaced the first boot, then turned around straddling it. Daddy put his other foot on my posterior to push while I began to pull and wrestle with the stubborn boot until it slipped off. That always happened suddenly, and when the boot came free, I went sprawling on the floor to our duet of rollicking laughter.

My interest in firearms was more than passive. At the age of eight Daddy humored my fascination with his target practice out by the pine woods by letting me try my hand at shooting a small-caliber pistol. I showed much more than average skill after only a few such outings. Daddy was surprised and delighted, and by the time I was ten I was a better shot with that pistol than any adult male in the area. Quite often one of the men from town out visiting Daddy would ask him to let Boop (that was my nickname) show her stuff with that pistol. I was good with a rifle, too. I loved the attention and my father's obvious pride in my prowess. So I always obliged them. But when I became a teen-ager I gave up my marksmanship. I was a woman then and women just didn't go around shooting bull's-eyes like Annie Oakley. Not in Plains.

Childhood memories of Christmas on the Carter farm are almost storybook perfect. What may have been missing in the mild winter climate of the south in the way of snow and sleigh bells was made up for in silvery, frost-laden pine boughs, the rich scent of cinnamon balls mingling with the more subtle aroma of holiday cookies and cakes being baked in the kitchen, and the happy sharing activities of friends and neighbors.

I remember how warm and lighthearted Daddy would be in late December. Through the year he worked so hard at the job of operating the farm profitably. By that time, he also had a peanut warehouse and an insurance business to run. But at Christmas time he seemed to shed his intensity. He took more time to talk to friends and employees. He always had his special recipe eggnog ready for those who made a practice of dropping in on Christmas morning to pay their respects. As a little girl, watching men come to see Daddy was an exciting annual event.

But Daddy didn't like the role of rural royalty. He sincerely loved people, and since his prominence and influence touched almost everyone, at Christmas time he tried to make personal contact with them.

Daddy's happiest moments during the annual Yule celebration were at the Elks' children's Christmas party he had inaugurated. Most of the farm children who lived in Sumter County were invited to the big holiday party each year on the Sunday before Christmas. Buses and cars that had volunteered for the day deposited their cargo of excited kids in front of the large rolling lawn at the Americus Elks Club. From as far back as I can remember Daddy expected me to be his assistant. Even after college days and marriage, I was there by his side as he lined up the children in front of the table laden with hot dogs, potato chips, lemonade, and ice cream. There was always more than they could eat. Then came the great moment for Daddy. With smiles which bubbled up from somewhere around his heart, he gave a gift to each child. Many were from poor families, and this would be their only gift, but by giving to all the children, the poor children were not singled out and embarrassed. By the end of the day, Daddy had received what was always his most treasured Christmas gift on the Elks Club lawn —adding a little happiness to a lot of children.

I was five when a minor plague stole the usual joy of the Christmas season from the three children then in our family. Jimmy, Gloria, and I came down with a fever, and red spots covered our bodies. Dr. Sam, our family physician, examined us, and it didn't take him long to diagnose the disease: severe, old-fashioned German measles. Dr. Sam instructed Mother to keep the shades drawn in the bedroom where we were to be quarantined. "And keep those kids in bed," he ordered. As a registered nurse and one of Dr. Sam's favorites, Mother knew before he told her what she would have to do. But she properly "yes sirred" him as he picked up his well-worn black bag, mumbled a Merry Christmas, and headed out the door.

Mother called in Annie Mae and instructed her to move Gloria's and my bed into Jimmy's bedroom and to fix the windows so no light could enter. She told her that light could damage our eyes because we had the measles. "You mean those poor babies are gonna spend Christmas in the dark?" Annie Mae protested. When she had finished blacking out the room, Jimmy, Gloria, and I were sent in to begin our confinement. We were placed in our beds and then the door was closed on the world of light and colors. I was glad my big brother and sister were somewhere in the gloom with me, but it felt like some awful punishment to be there.

The year before had been so different. Each year it was a Christmas Eve ritual for us to place a snack on the fireplace hearth for Santa. We certainly helped to keep him fat and jolly with a slice of Mother's popular Bourbon Lane cake filled with raisins and spices, a stack of holiday cookies all decorated with red and green frosting, and a tall glass of milk. It was also a tradition for us to search for a Christmas tree through our pine forest whose evergreen elegance refused to fade when the winter frost and wind dulled and stripped the rest of the countryside foliage. Daddy always went with us, and he would select and cut the most perfect seven-foot, long-needled pine he could find. Then we would haul it home and set it up in the dining room. But the year of the measles saw no such fun.

The days in the dark hobbled by. There was little that Jimmy, Gloria, and I wanted to say to each other, and less we could do. Each day I asked Mother how many days until Christmas, hoping there would be a reprieve from our sentence, but it was not to be. On the twenty-fourth, we were told by Dr. Sam that our fevers remained and we must stay in our limbo through Christmas Day. I cried. That night the dreadful thought seized me: What if Santa decided not to stop? What if he saw all the Carter children's bedroom lights off and thought we didn't live here anymore? I comforted myself by deciding that if he knew when I'd been bad or good, he would surely know I was entombed in Jimmy's room with the measles.

I also worried about whether Santa would go hungry. We hadn't laid out his midnight snack. Gloria assured me that Mother would take care of Santa. A sophisticated eight years old, she knew Mother took care of Santa every day. Sleep finally silenced my sad, anxious thoughts, and the next thing I remember was Mother gently caressing my brow and saying, "Ruth, wake up. It's Christmas morning." But all was still drowned in darkness. Mother sat me up in my bed and slipped my robe on me. Then she took my hand and led me across the room. Finally she lifted me up and placed me on a seat, and guided my hands to handle grips and my feet to pedals. I squealed with delight. It was the tricycle I had wanted for Christmas.

Mother did even more to bring some light into our darkened Christmas. On the night before she noticed that a string of lights was out on the tree. They were the old-fashioned kind of lights and if one burned out it extinguished the whole string. As Mother searched for the faulty bulb, she was thinking about her children and wishing she could give her ailing brood a truly merry Christmas. From the living room, where Daddy was assembling the bicycles for Jimmy and Gloria and the tricycle for me, came the strains of Christmas music from our battery-powered RCA console radio. Then Mother heard the announcer say that Little Jack Little, a nationally famous radio and vaudeville personality of that day, was in Atlanta for the holidays and would be singing over radio station WSB on Christmas day. A thought struck her. Could it be? No, it was too much to hope for. But the thought persisted and Mother went to bed with a prayer on her lips.

On Christmas eve, Mother called the Atlanta radio station and hesitantly asked to speak to Little Jack Little. Miraculously, his famous voice came on the phone and she explained her request. There was silence on the line for a moment. Then he said, "Let me see what we can do." Mother hung up the phone and sank against the wall quietly praying.

When Gloria, Jimmy, and I watched Mother and Daddy move the radio into our room, we wondered why they were doing it. "Merry Christmas," Mother said as she switched on the radio. "I thought you might like to listen to some Christmas carols."

The old radio hummed and then came the sound of music. It was nice of Mother to let us hear some Christmas songs, but we were not that interested until Little Jack Little's voice came over the loudspeaker. We began to listen, but we were still feeling the effects of our illness. Then, all of a sudden, Little Jack Little's voice boomed out, "And now I'm going to sing a song especially for three little Carter children who are ill: Jimmy, Ruth, and Gloria."

I sat up in bed and looked at Jimmy and Gloria. I couldn't believe it at first, nor could they. We stared at the radio as Mr. Little sang "Woodin Head, Puddin' Head Jones," a song we all loved. I began to giggle. Jimmy was smiling like sunshine and Gloria squealed with glee.

By now we were bouncing on our beds to the rhythm of the music, singing along with the bold voice of Mother's musical angel. She stood by the door with tears streaming down her face. Her prayer had been answered. Our melancholy Christmas had been made merry.

Our world of play out on the farm was for the most part what we created for ourselves. We had no playground, television, or movies and we rarely went into town for entertainment.

Jimmy, who as a boy went by the name "Hot," was constantly dreaming up some new project for the Carter kids and our black playmates. With a little help from the rest of us, he built a treehouse in the big chinaberry tree, and behind the house we made a high jump and pole-vaulting pit. Jimmy's biggest undertaking was when he decided to try to duplicate the ferris wheel we had enjoyed at the county fair. It proved to demand more engineering know-how and building material than we had. So it was never completed. But it was great fun trying over several months of Saturdays.

Daddy had a cute little playhouse built for Gloria and me. The playhouse was our most frequent place of entertainment, and for years Gloria, whose nickname was "Go Go," and I would retreat to it almost daily. We cooked on our orange crate stove and played with our dolls, serving them meals at our little table or tending all their needs in the delightful fantasy world we created inside those miniature four walls. After Billy was born and was able to sit up, he became our real live playhouse baby. It was such a treat to bring him there, prop him up in a doll chair and serve him from our little tea set.

Several times a year, Daddy treated us to a day in Americus, which is ten miles west of Plains. It usually began with a movie at the Rylander Theater and the feature was usually a western starring Gene Autry or Roy Rogers. After the picture we drove to the bakery. As we trooped in, the aroma was heavenly, and all those creamy, crusty, glazed, and buttered pastries and breads were so tantalizing. Our choice was always doughnuts, enough for our day on the town and some for breakfast the next morning. We ate our doughnuts as we window-shopped, an activity which was generally short but sweet with only three little department stores in town. Rarely would we buy anything; we just looked. The last place we went before we returned to the farm was the shop which sold hot-roasted pecans, peanuts, cashews, and chestnuts. Roasted nuts for our family was like carrying coals to Newcastle, but they were a favorite treat.

Every weekday the little yellow school bus would stop on the road next to our house and pick up Jimmy, Gloria, and me. A memory which I had successfully repressed until recently was the pain and guilt I felt when I looked back through the rear window of the bus and saw my black playmates walking to their school, a separate rundown all-black school, while we rode.

Our school, a red brick building, was located on a nameless street one block from where it intersected with the main street of downtown Plains. It was the cultural and activity center of our community as well as our school. Under its one roof the classes for all eleven grades were held. Grammar school went through the seventh grade; high school was the eighth through the eleventh.

If we received a good education, and we did, the primary reason was Miss Julia Coleman, the school superintendent. Miss Julia was a rare human being. Blind and crippled by polio, she lived a full life as a gifted educator. She had the ability to bring an appreciation of classical art, music, poetry, and literature to her pupils. As part of our education, Miss Julia asked different classes to create the scene of a famous painting. On the designated day, a large, life-size picture frame would be filled with live, costumed figures of students depicting the work of some great artist, and somehow a Renoir, a Rembrandt, or a Leonardo da Vinci painting would be magically transformed into something more than an ancient and obscure canvas. They became part of us. Miss Julia also submitted lists of recommended reading to each class, and at the end of the year, gold medals were awarded to the student in each class who completed and had submitted written reports on the largest number of books from her list. This motivation to read was greatly reinforced at home by Mother, and all of the Carter children became avid readers.

To Miss Julia separation of church and state was no excuse for separating the spiritual from the training of the child. Every school day began with Chapel, when each grade marched into the auditorium to the strains of some classical composer played on the piano by Miss Julia. A scripture passage was read and then repeated until all the students repeated it in unison. Special announcements were made and then we filed out to our classes to begin our schoolwork.

My best friend throughout my school years was a pretty brunette with liquid brown eyes named Rosalynn Smith. She lived in Plains in the gray clapboard house just four houses down the street from the Carter warehouse. She was a city girl and I lived out in the country, which made our constant companionship unusual. But Rosalynn's father, the town mechanic, was ill for years with leukemia, and when Mother went into town to provide her nursing service, I tagged along. On the night Mr. Smith died, Mother was attending him. She brought the grieving Rosalynn home to stay with me overnight, and soon we were almost inseparable. Just about every weekend I stayed at Rosalynn's home or she stayed with me at the farm. I enjoyed staying in town because it was near the school, and after Friday night activities we were within walking distance of the drugstore soda fountain where all our friends congregated. Rosalynn equally enjoyed staying at my house in the country. We rode the mule-drawn wagon Daddy used to pick up the produce in the fields or we rode our horses to nearby farms and stayed with my black friends.

The Pond House, a cottage built by Daddy on a little lake near the farm, was a favorite meeting spot for all our friends. It was furnished with a pool table, a Ping-Pong table, and an old jukebox. It was such fun to play songs without any need for nickels. Outside there was a barbecue and great fishing in the pond. The Pond House was the site chosen for most of our teen-age parties and school proms. With so few places to go, once we started dating in our teens, we usually ended up spending our evenings there. Today a new Pond House, built while Mother was in the Peace Corps in India, has become her home.

4

As the Twig
Is Bent

Although Daddy lavished his love and attention on me, I can remember feeling as a very small girl that he would love me just a little bit more if I were a boy. I believe that is the reason I tried harder than Gloria or Jimmy to please my father; why, for instance, his delight over my marksmanship with a pistol was so important to me. The pure pleasure that he found in his new baby son, Billy, seemed to confirm my feelings. But, strangely, I didn't resent his arrival. I was just happy that Daddy was happy. There were eight years separating Billy and me, which seems to have eliminated any sense of rivalry.

Mother was in poor health for several months after Billy's birth. Dr. Wise prescribed three cans of beer a day to enrich her milk and increase her strength. (One can hardly take the suggestion seriously, but it is bound to be made, that this natal conditioning is the explanation for Billy's adult consumption of that same prescription. His explanation, "I just like beer," seems more accurate.) During those first summer months, Gloria and I took turns caring for him so Mother could get the rest she needed. Of course, Annie Mae could have cared for him as she did when we were in school, but it was more play than work to us to do it ourselves.

One of Billy's first places of entertainment was under the family sewing machine. Gloria was the seamstress of the household, and when she went to work on the machine, Billy often crawled beneath it and watched her feet operate the treadle. He listened to the mesmerizing, pulsating whirr of the gears and bobbin, and the *chigg-chigg-chigg* of the sewing machine became the background for Billy's fantasies. He was driving a big car he told us, or running a tractor all by himself in his Daddy's fields.

At summer's end we went back to school and we relinquished him to Annie Mae. This sweet black lady, so quiet and gentle, loved and cared for him as if he had come from her own womb, just as she had loved Jimmy, Gloria, and me. Her humble grace was one of our deepest blessings.

Jack Clark was one of Billy's first black friends and an early masculine mentor. He lived in the large staff quarter house next to ours. Jack was the maintenance man for our house. There wasn't much that he couldn't fix, and he loved to talk. He taught Billy his first words, and he taught him not to wet his pants in a most unorthodox way. Every morning, during the chilly months, Jack built fires in the fireplaces of our house. Billy was usually on hand to watch the procedure, and if he happened to wet his pants, Annie Mae whisked him away to change him. She began to correct Billy mildly in his second year, and that was when Jack took over the potty-training chores. After he got a small fire going, he called his little charge over to the fireplace. "Now, little Billy," he said, "instead of wetting yourself, you just wet that fire and put it out." "Now, little Billy," Jack said, "what you did in that fire, you do in the toilet, not your pants." After a couple such lessons Billy realized that he could control his urinary fire extinguisher and relieve himself properly. Dr. Spock may never recommend this method, but it is hard to argue with such easy success.

From the time he was a toddler, Daddy took Billy with him whenever he could. As soon as he was old enough to walk and talk, they were almost inseparable. It was a familiar sight to see the two walking hand in hand from our house down the red dirt road through the orderly rows of pecan trees to the cotton and peanut fields. There was Daddy with his broad-brim straw hat shaped like a fedora, wearing bib khaki, and Billy dressed just like him. When they walked through the fields, Daddy inspected the cotton or peanut plants, and Billy, though not yet in school, was his apprentice.

There are striking physical similarities between my father and the man Billy grew to be. Daddy was short, stocky, ruddy complected. He wore glasses, the lenses were thicker than Billy's today. Daddy had poor eyesight, so poor that he could see very little without his glasses, but his eyes were a clear, bright, blue gray. When he was angry, however, they seemed to change to a steel gray and they had an ominous sparkle. I recall that I feared Daddy's silent anger more than a beating. One look chilled me to the heart. But he was usually carefree and loved good times. He wasn't giddy. His enjoyment of life was low-keyed, and in his later years, there was nothing he enjoyed more than his relaxed times with his youngest child.

They strode into the fields the day the cotton plants were white with blooms. "Billy," Daddy instructed, "these flowers won't live very long. Tomorrow they'll be sort of a reddish color. The next day they'll fall off."

Billy wasn't that interested in the life cycle of a cotton blossom, but he was interested in who was telling him about it. If Daddy said it, it must be important. He watched his thick-framed father kneel down and hold a bloom like it was the face of a child, so Billy knelt down and held one, too. In his earliest memories, he recalls how much he wanted to grow up to be just like this man, Mr. Earl.

"When the flower falls off," Daddy went on, "it leaves this." He pointed to the round green seed pod at the base of the flower. "That's where the cotton grows." Months later he brought Billy out to the fields and showed him the pod again. Now it was brown and split open, exposing its cargo of fluffy down. Billy loved it because it was Daddy's world.

As they strolled through the peanut fields, Daddy showed Billy the green peanut pods and explained that as they grow, the plant stalk bends downward and pushes the pods into the earth. "When they're ready, we'll dig them out of the ground." On later inspections, Billy recalled how Daddy pulled a plant out of the soil and shook the dirt from it to see how the peanuts were maturing. Now he knew a little more about these good-tasting nuts. All he had known until then was that they were best of all boiled in the shells in salt water, but he couldn't eat too many of them or he would get sick. Walking with Daddy down the furrows between the peanut plants, Billy tried to put his feet where his father had left footprints in the soft red soil. He couldn't reach them, but he stubbornly leaped from footprint to footprint until he was so tired that Daddy had to carry him home.

By the time Billy was old enough to work with his father, Daddy wasn't doing manual labor as he had when Jimmy was a boy. But Billy did get a feel for farming, a love of it. He was a confirmed son of the soil and always would be. But the little towhead could never have imagined, nor could his father, though he knew how to dream big, that Carter Peanuts, years later, would be known all over the world, and that Billy's own expertise as a peanut merchant would free his older brother to run for political office. That is the role that Billy would play one day, and those father-and-son strolls and conversations were where his abilities were first nurtured.

When Billy was only three years old, Jimmy left home to go to Georgia Southwestern College, and from there he went to Georgia Tech, and then the Naval Academy. That left Billy as the only son of the household—the baby, and his family of older sisters and parents had a great time spoiling him. Gloria was his number one pacifier. If he began to cry, both Gloria and I would run to console him, and when a kiss or hug failed, she was called upon to rock him in our squeaky, old highback rocking chair. That always seemed to soothe his bruised body or psyche when nothing else could. After he started school, I took him to his first-grade classroom each morning, and when he got out at the end of the school day, I was always there to meet him and walk with him to the bus we called Cracker Box for the ride home. None of us had any idea we were denying Billy the right to learn how to take care of himself.

Daddy tried to cushion Billy's life, too. I recall the Sunday morning when Billy had no coat for Sunday School. Daddy searched through his closet and found several of his jackets, but Billy complained that they looked like old folks' clothes. Mother said that one of them would surely be all right for one Sunday, but Daddy interceded. "Lillian," he said, "when you love pretty clothes as much as Buckshot [Daddy's nickname for Billy] and you don't have any pretty clothes, it doesn't matter how many clothes you have, you don't have anything to wear."

Jimmy, who had known firm discipline while he was growing up, was less patient with Billy. One Sunday morning we were all getting ready for Sunday School, and three-year-old Billy was dressed in a little navy blue suit with a white starched shirt and bright red tie. Jimmy, then a high school senior, was told to put some brilliantine on his little brother's unruly blond hair and comb it. But when he reached for Billy, he jerked away. Jimmy grabbed him but he couldn't calm his brother who was acting quite bratty. In disgust, Jimmy threw Billy faceup across his lap and said, "If you don't want it on your hair, I'll give you some to drink." With no serious intent of making Billy actually drink the oil, he shook the bottle above his mouth. As he did, the top accidentally fell off and the hair oil poured over Billy's face and drenched his shirt and suit.

Daddy exploded and Jimmy got a severe reprimand.

But that kind of dark moment was rare. Billy's preschool days on the farm were usually happy days, catching frogs, hunting, fishing, and playing with his friends who were the children of the farmhands. Sometimes he could coax one of the older men to let him sit on the back of one of the eight horses we owned. Billy loved to wander around the fences and pens where the horses, goats, sheep, cows, and pigs were kept in our barnyard, but his favorite animals were Pete and Reet, our pet squirrels. They usually stayed out on the screened front porch where he would coax them on to his hand and let them run up over his shoulders and scamper up and down his body.

A physically sweet experience for all the Carter children was the making of sugar cane syrup on the farm. After the cane had reached maturity in the fall of the year, it was cut and hauled to the vat yard out behind the barn. Mules powered a turnstile attached to a gear system which operated the cane crusher. The cane was placed in a hopper which fed it through the metal rollers of the crusher and the sugar-laden juice squeezed from the stalks dropped out of a spiggot into a large cast-iron kettle. All the children were on hand to watch this process, and from time to time we were allowed to sample the sweet, golden juice. It was like a visit to the candy factory. A wood fire burned under the kettle, and a mule-powered paddler kept the juice stirring. Finally, after six or seven hours, it reached the right consistency. Then the serious business began of drawing off the syrup into tin half-gallon and gallon containers with the Carter label.

We had another treat in store. On the evening of the syrup

making, we gathered in the kitchen to make taffy. Daddy, who loved to assume the role of chef, always presided over this sweet-tooth happy hour. He hovered over a pan on the stove, and when he thought the syrup had thickened properly, he put a drop of it in a glass of cold water. If it congealed into a spindly string, that indicated it was right for the taffy pull. Daddy then said, "Gather round." He poured the pasty syrup on a strip of wax paper, and after it cooled, he gave each of us blobs of the hardening goo. We took partners, and sharing a piece of taffy, began to pull, folding the stretched candy into a small size and then pulling again. In a while the amorphous mass of sweetness turned white and stiffened. When it was hard enough, Daddy took the taffy (we called it syrup candy), cut it up into pieces, and served each of us delicious morsels.

The Fourth of July on the Carter farm was the high feast day of the year, inaugurated by Daddy as a way of saying "Thank you" to all the people who worked on the land. It was the biggest barbecue in the county. Whole pigs were placed on large logs over a barbecue pit and were roasted all night long until they were cooked to smokey, succulent, golden-brown perfection. The main cooking was usually done by Daddy. By morning, the pigs were just beginning to sizzle, and melting fat dropped into the coals, causing smoke to curl up from the fire, wafting the hunger-teasing scent of barbecued pork everywhere. Tables were set up all across the lawn and covered with clean white cloths. Near noontime the roast pigs were ready, and other dishes were brought out from the kitchen where Annie Mae, Rachael, and Bertha Mae had been helping Mother all morning. A brunswick stew which Daddy prepared ahead of time was sure to be served. It was his special recipe: ground chicken, pork and beef, flavored with tomatoes, corn, and spices slowly simmered into a thick stew. Daddy toiled over his gastronomic creation for almost twenty-four hours. It was really a meal in itself, but we always had it as a side dish to the barbecue. Slaw, corn on the cob, pickles and relish, cakes, pies, and all the lemonade we could drink were also part of our Fourth of July menu.

In the late morning hours, everything was finally ready, and the hired hands began to arrive in horse-drawn wagons. Close neighbors were invited, too. By mealtime, there were usually, two hundred happy and hungry men, women, and children gathered for the feast. It was always a joyous occasion for everyone.

There was one festivity Billy liked even more than the Fourth of July: hog killing. On the day of the first frost, early in the morning before dawn, all the farmhands gathered under the flickering glow of kerosene lanterns to begin two long, hard days of work. Over fifty pigs had to be slaughtered and everything from country ham and pork loins to sausage, souse, and pigs' feet would be processed. There was plenty for everyone to do. Although Billy was never afraid to duck out of hard work when he was a little lad, he enjoyed scurrying about carrying wood to fuel the fire under the boiling pots of lard and chittlins, or following the men who carried meat to the grinder for sausage. The most pleasurable thing about the day for him was that he was excused from school by his parents and he could indulge in his favorite pastime—being near his Daddy.

The children were never allowed near the barn during the actual slaughter. By the time we arrived, big pots were filled with water and already boiling on open fires. Makeshift tables were set up, and the hogs were hung from beams where they were cleaned and dressed with precision by experienced hands. The entrails were cleaned and boiled, and then used as skin for sausage. That was Daddy's project and usually Billy's lot was to keep the pieces of pork squeezed down into the hand-cranked grinder with a wooden pestle as Daddy turned the grinder handle. The ground pork was then stuffed into the skins. It never took all the entrails to make the sausage, so at the end of the processing the help took home livers, kidneys, and the extra cuts of meat.

The second day was spent salting down hams and putting them in the smokehouse behind the big house. Racks were made in the smokehouse on which to hang the sausage, hams, and shoulders. Other meat was put into the cold storage locker in downtown Plains. It would all be a part of the farm's daily fare throughout the following year. I believe that is why hog killing felt like a working celebration. Thanksgiving Day is rather vague in the memories of the Carter children. This was our Thanksgiving. It spoke of abundance, provision, and prosperity, not in gold, but in bread. Daddy rarely mentioned his faith. But there was an air of gratitude in his spirit as he oversaw these days of animal harvest which told us he knew it was God who had blessed him so. As for the little boy who followed him around, he wasn't awfully concerned about theology either. He just hoped God was as good as his Daddy.

Just a little piece down the red dirt road from our house on the farm was a weather-stained, brown wood box of a building, standing on the other side of our barn. It was the home of the Berrys, one of the several black families employed by my father. Theirs was quite a different world from ours. It wasn't the caricatured world of the white master and cowering black subjects, but there was segregation, prejudice, and even insensitivity in our little community which would have to yield to a better way. But there was also so much that was real and beautiful with that centuries-old way of life. That beauty was never more clearly seen than in the close association and deep affection found between black and white children.

Bishop was the son of David and Bertha Mae Berry. He was

Billy's best friend and constant playmate. From shortly after birth they were inseparable buddies. Segregate schools, churches, buses—nothing could segregate these two little boys who loved each other. Their appearance together brought delighted smiles from all but the meanest of the local rednecks as they watched little Billy walking down the dusty road with Bishop. When Daddy drove his pickup truck into town, if Billy was riding in the bed of the truck, there was Bishop always beside him, sometimes laughing or seriously talking, but always engrossed in one another or the activities they shared. They ate most of their meals together, though Bishop wasn't permitted to sit at the dining room table. That was off limits to blacks. Annie Mae prepared their meal and served it at a separate little table which stood in the kitchen between the wood-burning stove and the woodpile on one side, and the entrance to the back screen porch on the other. There Billy and Bishop ate dinner almost every night.

Billy's home was the farm and his family included the many black friends he had, not just Bishop. Another important black child in Billy's youth was A. D. David, who was Jimmy's age and had been his closest friend as he grew up. After Jimmy left home for college and the Navy, A. D. often acted as the overseer of all the little black and white children on the farm. In fact, A. D. was one more family member who pampered Billy. Billy has been teased all his life that he never really learned to talk until he went to school because A. D. had taken care of his every need before it had to be expressed.

Annie Mae was A. D.'s first cousin. She was Mother's maid before Billy was born and now she was our favorite baby-sitter. When Mother and Daddy went out for the evening, Annie Mae, A. D., and Bishop came up to the big house to take care of us. Annie Mae was still in her teens, but the myopia of youth made her seem like an older woman to us. We all stood peeping out of the window, anxiously awaiting Mother and Daddy's departure to their frequent evening activities and parties. "They're gone!" we shouted when we saw the big family Oldsmobile pull out of the driveway. Then we all rushed to the front bedroom. I never knew when we were young why Annie Mae always chose that particular room for what followed next, but looking back, it seems clear that it was because this was the one room where she could see the driveway out of the window and spot my parents' car should they unexpectedly return.

The fire would already be lit in the bedroom fireplace, and after we had all settled down, there came the magic moment, the event filled with terror and delight. One of us ran over to the light switch and turned out the lights. Then Annie Mae began to chant in a quavering voice which sounded like a voice from the grave, "All good chillin better gather 'round 'cause there's a good, strange thing's gonna happen tonight." We huddled together in the total darkness, waiting for the spell of this benevolent black sorceress to terrorize us. Gloria usually held Billy closely to her because he always screamed the loudest when the scariest moments came, though I can't say he was ever more frightened than the rest of us, just more vocal.

When Annie Mae spoke again, it was a whining, high-pitched voice. She told us scary stories of ghosts and goblins that ate little white children who didn't mind, and cursed the folks who worked on Sunday. At the right hair-raising, blood-curdling moment, she fell silent. I could feel my heart and hear my breath. In the silence, Annie Mae quietly stole through the room toward the fireplace. We couldn't see her, but we could hear her movements through the darkness of the room. Suddenly, we saw a red glow begin to flutter and bob in the fireplace. The glowing light seemed to levitate from the bed of coals and float around the room, darting toward one of us and then another. This is when Billy began to squirm. Then he whimpered, and, finally, as the fiery demon approached him, he broke into wild screams. Gloria held him even closer, as much for her comfort as his. When the ruby light began to fade, it floated slowly back toward the fireplace and settled once again back into the ashes. As frightening as it was, this was the entertainment we all liked best.

Childhood mystery usually must yield to adult perception, and years later Annie Mae told us how she had created the greatest show on earth. She carefully prepared the fire early enough to allow coals to form, red and radiant. Then when we were all ready she took one of the embers in her spittle-dampened fingers and nimbly placed it between her teeth. As she quickly breathed on it, it glowed brightly, and then she danced around the room, scaring us half to death. Ziegfeld, P. T. Barnum, or Houdini had nothing on our Annie Mae.

Her performance with the live coal was always followed by story time. Our favorite was the story of "Ol' Joe" who made the mistake of going fishing on a Sunday. That day he caught a fish, and as soon as it was on the hook, it began to speak. It said, "Pull me up, Joe. Pull me up, Joe, my sickened soul, my sickened soul." Joe pulled it up, and in prose and poetry, Annie Mae unfolded the plot step by step. We all knew what was coming next. We had heard the story many times before, but like a favorite meal, we always delightfully anticipated each morsel. Joe took the fish home, cleaned it, cooked it, and ate it, and before each action the fish chanted, "Take me home, Joe. Clean me, cook me, eat me," repeated to the awful end. But because Ol' Joe caught the fish on Sunday, at the end when the meal was finished, his belly suddenly popped open. The fish was freed from Ol' Joe's stomach, like the story of Jonah and the Whale in reverse, then gathered up his scattered parts, went into the yard to retrieve his entrails and scales, and ran to the creek and jumped back in. This morality play influenced our attitude toward Sunday activities for years. I can recall my own deep guilt feelings about fishing on Sunday which came from Annie Mae's story. Years later, when Billy was falsely accused of illegally selling beer on Sunday, I doubt that he thought of the curse of Ol' Joe, but the shadow of Annie Mae's blue-law morality came back to haunt him for a few days.

The years have faded many memories, but we have never forgotten these early relationships with our friends on the farm, whatever their race. If Billy saw color, it was chiefly in reaction to the prejudice which was so foreign to the experience of his heart, or in an effort to maintain his image: redneck Billy the Kid, shoot-from-the-hip bigot.

When Jimmy was governor of Georgia, one of his most trusted state patrolmen was Officer Freeman, who was a walking testimonial to the affirmation that "Black is beautiful." It was apparent that, in his case, black was tall, strong, and very competent, too. In the line of duty, Officer Freeman accompanied Jimmy on his frequent weekend trips to his home in Plains. But when he was off duty, he headed for Billy's home. He knew he was always welcome there, but some of the white patrolmen teased him about it. "What would the white folks of Plains say if they knew you were down at Billy's eating at his table and acting white?" they'd jest. Officer Freeman always laughed with them. He knew they respected him, and he knew they were right about many of the local "white folks." But he didn't feel black or white with Billy. He just felt like a human being.

One evening when Officer Freeman was having supper at Billy's, Billy put in his humorous dig at local bigotry—as usual at his own expense. Everyone was laughing and joking, and Billy turned to his black guest and said, "Freeman, you're welcome to eat at my table any day, but do you see that broom over there in the corner? Well, just relax unless that doorbell rings, and if any of my friends from Plains drop by, you jump up and start sweeping like hell!''

In 1966 Billy financed a lawsuit in Georgia which sought to ban segregation in private schools. The segregationist forces, which included his cousin Hugh Carter, bitterly opposed his action, but what he had experienced with Bishop and A. D. was thicker than blood. And, anyway, he knew he was fighting for what was right. Billy might not feel at home in a freedom march, but he had his own effective way to strike a blow for the blacks he knew were his equals.

5

Behind Every Great Man

Jimmy showed unusual discipline and industry through his high-school years. And he frequently demonstrated the courage, sometimes the feistiness, of his convictions. When Gloria broke her left wrist on the schoolground because of the cruel roughhousing of a boy much bigger than Jimmy was, he didn't hesitate to come to his sister's defense. He plowed into her assailant with the ferocity of an underweight bantam rooster. But on another occasion when Gloria *hit him with a wrench,* he took his BB gun and plinked her on the behind.

Jimmy did more than dream about the Naval Academy. He repeatedly reviewed the academic requirements in the Academy catalog. Daddy began sending letters in Jimmy's senior year to our district congressman, requesting that Jimmy be considered for his recommendation to Annapolis. Jimmy's chief concern was that he might not be able to pass the rigid physical requirements for entrance. He weighed only 128 pounds and he had flat feet. He stuffed himself at the table, worked out with weights in the backyard in an effort to gain weight, and kept a Coke bottle in his bedroom on which he would roll the bottoms of his feet in an effort to strengthen them.

He was a serious student, or more accurately, he enjoyed school work and the more challenging the better. He was also beginning to prove his business abilities. These were the war years, but except for hometown boys leaving in greater numbers to enter the service, Plains was little affected by World War II. But farm prices did begin to soar, and when the price of a bale of cotton went up to $1.29 per pound, Jimmy sold the bales he had bought for a nickel a pound years earlier. With the profit, he then bought five tenant shacks which brought in $16.50 a month in rent. The townspeople began to talk about how young Jimmy had inherited his Daddy's business instinct.

During this same time Daddy developed an innovation in the marketing of peanuts. In the past the farmers had sold their peanut crops directly to the peanut oil companies. Daddy became a wholesale agent for the farmers, buying their peanut crops at a good market price and then selling them to the peanut oil companies. As a part of this business expansion, he had built the Carter warehouse.

Jimmy worked for Daddy after school and during vacations, but then he left home for Georgia Southwestern College, and in 1943, after a year at Georgia Tech, he received his appointment to the Naval Academy. I was fourteen and my best friend, Rosalynn, was sixteen when he came home from Annapolis on his first school break. He didn't pay too much attention to us; we were just girls and Jimmy was a big Naval Academy midshipman. He was friendly enough when he happened to bump into us in the kitchen or downtown; "Hi, Ruth. Hi, Rosalynn," he said and then off he would go wherever busy midshipmen go when at home in Plains. Then just three days before he was to return to the Academy after almost a month at home, the girl he was dating left for Florida. He had nothing to do that night, so he asked me to go to a movie in Americus with him. I told him I already had a date but I suggested that he ask Rosalynn to go with him and we could make it a double date. That night Jimmy learned that Rosalynn was no longer a little girl. The young woman whose father had died three years earlier had a lot of maturity and beauty that he had been slow to see.

The four of us drove to the movie in Americus. I don't remember what we saw, and the rest of the evening wasn't particularly eventful, but for Jimmy it was a history-making night. He dated Rosalynn the next two nights alone. He has never divulged any particulars concerning those two dates, but obviously Rosalynn had torpedoed his bachelor boat. He was absolutely moonstruck, and he proposed before returning to school. Rosalynn told him she wasn't sure, but when Jimmy came home again for the Washington's Birthday break, they became engaged. After his graduation from Annapolis, they were married in the Plains Methodist Church on July 7, 1946. The Smiths had always been Methodists, but when Rosalynn married Jimmy she became a Baptist.

The wedding was simple but beautiful. It was a very emotional moment for me. I was overcome at one point that my two best friends had come together, yet, at the same time, I felt I was losing them both—to each other. They were moving away from Plains after the wedding to begin a new life in the navy. As they knelt before the altar to exchange their vows of commitment, I was unable to hold back my tears.

Billy was eight the year Jimmy and Rosalynn were married. That same year Daddy's peanut warehouse became a part of Billy's life, and he began doing chores there after school. It was the world he liked best, the one he felt most at home in. He learned to work hard, not because he had to, but because he knew Daddy was a hard worker and respected other hard-working people. That was motivation enough.

Daddy rarely pushed or corrected his youngest employee, but Billy didn't feel like the boss's son when it came to doing his job. He felt he had to prove himself, and he did. As he grew older, he began loading heavy sacks and learning the ropes of the warehouse business from field hauling, grading, shelling, and sacking to distribution and sales. He was developing a sinewy, broad-shouldered body. He was pulling down a man's wage and earning it.

These were some of Billy's happiest times. Between the farm, his school chums, and his haven in the warehouse, his days were full and pleasant. His major unhappiness was school. Although he was very bright, he seemed to be resisting the image of all the other Carter children. Jimmy, Gloria, and I all excelled in school. Billy seemed bent on not being a Carter cliché. He also had a problem with stuttering. It was not very pronounced unless he got excited. Then he sometimes could barely get a complete sentence out. He was encouraged to overcome his stuttering by reading aloud before a lighted candle; if the candle blew out he knew he was stuttering. This didn't dampen his interest in reading, but it did little to cure his stuttering or improve his school work.

In 1948, two years after Jimmy and Rosalynn were married, Daddy decided to do something he had always wanted to do: build Mother the dream house she had always longed for. He chose a large and lovely sight right in the middle of Plains where he could have a lot of grass and lawn. But the house was going to be exactly as Mother wanted it. He took great pride in building our new house. Both he and Mother were very excited about it. It was built of virgin timber from trees on one of the first farms Daddy owned in Webster County, and he carefully selected each board. For the living room, he chose one kind of wood; for the dining room, another. Each room was built with loving care. He planned the house so Billy could have the whole upstairs to himself. I told Daddy I wanted lots of closet space and a sun deck off my room. Billy just thought it was neat that he could have the upstairs all to himself.

Billy was eleven when the family moved to town. It was only two miles from the old place to our new house in Plains, but with the move Billy said good-bye to the farm life he loved. He was leaving all his farm friends and neighbors. He moved two miles into a totally different world. Billy was almost a teen-ager, but he was still Daddy's frequent companion. In fact, the only advantage Billy felt in the move to town was that he could spend more time with Daddy at the office and warehouse.

In 1949, our first year in town, Daddy ran for the Georgia State Legislature. Twelve-year-old Billy was active in his campaign. He passed out cards on the street and rode with Daddy as he went around the district shaking hands. After he won the election and went to Atlanta, he often took Billy with him to serve as a page in the legislature. But even with all that excitement, Billy missed the farm and became awfully lonely for his old buddies. He had little opportunity to see them anymore, but rising adolescent passion and providence changed his bleak feelings.

Sybil Spires was a new girl in town; that is, she wasn't a native of the area, and anyone not born in Plains was new. She had moved from Eufaula, Alabama, in 1948, when she was eight years old. Billy had been aware of the pretty little girl with the long blond curls for some time, but now that he was in his teens, and Sybil was growing older and prettier all the time, he made a point of getting better acquainted with her. As someone has observed, it only takes a spark to get a fire going. This one was destined to be a four-alarmer!

One beautiful spring afternoon, the bell rang marking the end of the school day, and one hundred and thirty-five lively young spirits poured out of the school building exit into the bright, warm afternoon sun. It was twelve-year-old Sybil's daily routine to go down to her dad's barber shop on the main street of Plains to sweep and clean up the day's accumulation of clippings and trash. Her wage was a nickel, which she usually spent moments later for a Coke at Dr. Godwin's drugstore down on the corner.

When Sybil left school that day, she took the shortcut through the softball field and up a three-foot sloping embankment to the sidewalk which led into town just a few blocks away. She was walking faster than usual because she wanted to get through her cleanup chores. The afternoon was too nice to waste indoors. As she slowed her pace to turn into the barber shop, she felt a strong hand on each shoulder.

"Sweetheart, how are you?" She recognized the familiar voice of Mr. Earl Carter, the only one she knew who called her "sweetheart." As he turned her around, she gave him the warm embrace which usually accompanied their greeting.

"Why don't you go with me, Miss Lillian, and Billy to the baseball game tonight?" he asked.

That sounded so exciting, but since she was only twelve Sybil wondered if her mother would let her go. After all, Billy was almost fourteen, and she wasn't sure her mother would let her date an older man. But then maybe she would, since Mr. Earl had invited her, and he and Miss Lillian would be taking her.

Her mother said yes, and that was Billy's first date with Sybil. The most memorable moment wasn't the game between the two teams in Albany, or the thrill of a night out with a real, live young man; it was the popcorn. Boxes and boxes of popcorn. By the end of nine innings, Sybil was sure she was dying of popcornitis. She had never seen anyone eat so much popcorn as Billy had. It was her first exposure to two facets of her future husband's psyche: generosity and overindulgence.

Later, when they were both in high school, Billy asked Sybil to ride to a basketball game with him. Since she was playing on the girls' team, Sybil was expected to ride on the bus with the team, but she wanted to ride with Billy, so she agreed to meet him after school at the gym door just as soon as she had time to get permission from the principal to go with him. But when she met Billy, she had to deliver the bad news that the principal wouldn't give his permission. Billy was furious. He drew his fist back and drove it through the glass window on the gym door.

It was Sybil's first exposure to another part of Billy's complex personality: his temper. She just stood there looking with consternation at her furious friend. No one but Billy knew how much she cared for this volcanic boy even though he sometimes left her bewildered and anxious.

In the fall of 1952, the whole family was together for a visit and we went to the Flint River for a meal at a restaurant which specialized in Daddy's favorite, fried catfish. He sat drawn and pale before a platter of fried fish. He took a couple of bites and then apologized, "I feel sick to my stomach. I'm afraid I can't eat any more." In that moment I knew something was terribly wrong with Daddy. I left the restaurant shaken, and I realize now that I sensed he was critically ill but couldn't bring myself to express consciously what my heart knew. Some months later, on July 22, 1953, he was gone.

I had traveled frequently from Fayetteville, North Carolina, where I lived after my marriage, to what has always been home —Plains. My primary reason was to visit my parents. Daddy was as special to me as he was to Billy. I truly thought of him as the finest, the greatest! Yes, I can use that word, the greatest man I have ever known. I don't consciously recall the day when I lay in my crib at the age of eight months hovering near death. But I was told by my mother that when the doctor informed Daddy I was dying and there was nothing more he could do, Daddy went to my crib, removed the intravenous tubes from my fever-ravaged body, picked me up in his arms on a pillow, and carried me to the window. There he held me and implored God to save his baby daughter's life. I lived. And for that, and for other reasons too deep to fathom, I felt a consuming love for my father all my early life.

Daddy's death was not an unexpected tragedy for just our family. The whole town, and countless people across the state, expressed their grief on the passing of this man. Earl Carter had a big heart, and he had shared it with many people.

We should have expected his death. But we never did. Even after months of lingering illness, his spirit was so full of life, no one really believed that he wouldn't get well. Even after the diagnosis was final—terminal cancer—Daddy instructed the family to laugh and be happy around the house. "If someone comes over and they act sad and you think you have to act sad for them, go ahead. But when they leave, please try to be happy. I love to hear you laugh." He had no time for self-pity.

It sounds brash, but Carter determination is almost invincible. When Carters set their minds to do something, it just gets done. Jimmy's amazing, successful presidential race is only the most recent and best publicized example of this trait. Daddy was no less determined, and we were so sure that he would win his fight against cancer that it made his death all the more unexpected.

Jimmy returned to Plains for the funeral and he was given the task of going out into the county and notifying all our friends and neighbors of Daddy's death. I went along with him. Most of the farmers had no telephones, so we trudged across one field after another to speak to them. I especially remember Ed, a big black man who responded with uncontrolled grief. He shouted out in pain and fell across the steering wheel of his tractor sobbing. Other people felt equal sorrow. Only Daddy and many sharecroppers and widows knew his generosity. We found out only after his death of his many sizable and secret gifts to others. People stepped forward with stories of his charitable acts which he had asked them never to tell. Some told of income he had supplemented; others told of scholarships their young children had for college training. Many black sharecroppers who had bought their own land were able to do so only because Earl Carter took their word as collateral.

Jimmy has always been equipped with a steel will, and he had left Plains determined to become the best officer that the Naval Academy could produce. He did not leave home because of a conflict with his father. They had their clashes, but potent personalities usually clash if they are to maintain their individuality. They were both powerful men. These two streams couldn't possibly flow in the same channel. Jimmy had to seek his own destiny away from Plains. He deeply respected Daddy, but now Jimmy discovered that his father had a hidden benevolence and compassion for people that he had not seen in his youth and had omitted from his own life. It was a new insight into his father's character that influenced Jimmy's own approach to people.

Billy left the house early on the day after Daddy's death. No one could find him. He didn't return home until it was almost dark and we all had become very concerned. Billy had a lot of crying and screaming to do, but he also had an errand to run. He came into the house calling for Mother. She was in the back sitting room where, with my sister, Gloria, she had been receiving the condolences of relatives most of the day. Billy knocked on the door and then walked in.

"Mother," he said, "I've brought you a gift so you won't be so lonely now that Daddy's gone." He reached out to her. There cradled in his hands was a little green parakeet. "I hope he learns to talk real soon," he said.

We had all been caught up in our personal grief over Daddy's

death. But it was Billy who felt the hurt and grief that Mother
was experiencing. He had traveled most of the day looking for
that little bird. When he couldn't find one in Americus, he took
the long trek to Albany. He put in a lot of miles just to buy a
pet for his grieving mother. He may have been the youngest of
us, but in that hour of sorrow, he proved the most thoughtful.

Reconstructing life with Daddy gone was slow and painful
and sometimes frightening for Mother and Billy. An unfortu-
nate part of human nature is that we rarely know how much
someone means to us until we lose him. Mother had always
seemed very strong and independent, but it soon became clear
that her strength had been sustained by her husband. He had
nourished her heart, had been her reason for living. With his
death, that reason was gone. She slipped into a depression that
she could not seem to escape. Her children's attention, the
encouragement of friends, activity, even medication—nothing
could lift her out of her darkness.

Billy's lifelong dream had been to work in his father's business. Many times, as he and Daddy rode over the farms in the
late afternoon, Daddy would say to him, "Buckshot, someday
you'll be in charge of things when you grow up. Jimmy's chosen
the navy and you've chosen the land." It didn't quite work out
that way. In his will Daddy left a sizable accumulation of bonds
and the downtown property to Mother, which included the
warehouse business. All the farms were to be divided equally
among the four children and Mother. But she was a nurse, not
a business woman. Although we since have learned that she,
too, can do just about anything she sets her mind to doing, in
the state of depression to which she descended after Daddy's
funeral, she could never have handled the responsibilities of the
family business. His father's early death precluded the possibility of Billy's taking over. He was only fifteen. Jimmy was called
home to run the business.

It was a difficult decision for Jimmy to make. His future in the navy looked extremely promising. He was deep into nuclear submarine development, and no doubt he would have become an admiral and contributed much to naval engineering and administration. But he decided to return to Plains. Rosalynn was upset. She wanted Jimmy to remain in the navy. They had a good life. Someone else could take care of the business and besides, she would be faced with the smalltown world of Plains and the inevitable personality conflicts with close relatives. She wanted no part of it. No, she would not go home! But after the tears, anger, and disappointment let up somewhat, she reluctantly agreed to return.

It was not easy for Jimmy either. When he finally resigned his commission and came home, Mother agreed to go into partnership with him. He bought approximately a forty-percent interest in the business, and he and Rosalynn with their three small sons—Jack, Chip, and Jeffery—moved into a little thirty dollars-a-month apartment which allowed them some privacy from relatives. They both went to work at the warehouse. Jimmy did most of the manual labor while Rosalynn weighed trucks, kept the books, and did much of the other office work. The peanut business was completely new to Jimmy, and when he started looking into the accounts receivable, he found a set of books that only Daddy could have deciphered. There was no way of telling who owed what. So, the first year the peanut business grossed $187.

Daddy's death was hardest of all on Billy. In his own way, his grief equaled Mother's, and most of it he bore alone. He couldn't go to Mother. He saw how broken she was. There was no one else he wanted to share his pain with—except maybe Sybil.

Billy and Sybil weren't simply friends. Sybil, though young, became his mother, counselor, and companion. They were inseparable. She would sit with Billy while he studied, and they always ate lunch at school together. They filled their days with each other. I think Sybil was the only one who really knew the extent of Billy's grief. He carefully hid it from everyone else.

Another change was in store for Billy. Arrangements had been made even before Daddy died to send Billy to Gordon Military School in Barnesville, Georgia. So at fifteen he left the home he loved in Plains and found himself in an alien atmosphere of uniforms and military discipline. It wasn't all hardship by any means. He had his moments of pleasure, and one of them occurred on his first trip home from Gordon. Billy walked down Main Street in his gray uniform with its brass buttons and gold-frilled shoulder straps, and though clothes may not make a man, a uniform on an old, familiar frame can make a maiden's heart warm twenty degrees. When he walked into the drugstore where Sybil was sipping on her daily Coke, she saw more than her good buddy Billy. She saw a handsome young man and her fourteen-year-old heart was smitten.

"Hi, Billy." Her voice couldn't conceal her joy, but she felt embarrassed. She wanted to pull the words back and say them again more calmly so that the whole world wouldn't know how crazy she was about that general who stood there smiling at her as though he had just won the Civil War. Billy *had* won a major campaign in the South. Sybil Spires was his. As they walked out of the drugstore together, the girl who had been his friend was his sweetheart, and that is the way it has been ever since.

The next day, Sybil went uptown with her mother to the drugstore to have a prescription filled. Billy was standing at the counter as they walked in, and when he saw Mrs. Spires, that Carter determination asserted itself.

"Miss Lucille," Billy said, "why don't you give Sybil to me?"

"Billy, do you really want her?"

"Yes, ma'am, Miss Lucille. I really do."

"Well, okay, Billy," she said. "I'll give you an I.O.U. right now."

With rare maternal understanding and trust, Mrs. Spires picked up the drugstore charge pad from the counter and tore out a sheet. On the back of it she wrote, "I, Lucille Spires, do hereby give my daughter, Sybil, to Billy Carter." It was prophetic.

Billy returned to Gordon Academy, but not for long. When he came home for Thanksgiving, he told his mother, "I just can't leave you again. You need me too much." What he meant was, I need you, but he was trying to be a man, so it came out, "You need me."

Returning home didn't do much to ease Billy's pain. He still felt self-conscious and alone. The first day he re-enrolled at the high school, it was almost as though he had quit and was forced to start over. The questioning of his classmates heightened his anxiety. "Why'd you leave the military school, Billy?" "I just didn't like it there." "Hey, Billy, you're back. What happened?" "Nothin'. I just didn't like the damn school." In a few days the questions subsided, but Billy's malaise continued. When he walked in the door after school, the house was either empty without Mother there or empty with her there. She was trying hard to conceal the shadow of death on her heart, but it showed. Billy tried going to the warehouse more often, but that was even worse. Instead of Daddy, there was Jimmy, all friendly and brotherly, and all business. Jimmy was consumed with the task of learning the business and running it. Billy tried to stay away from the warehouse but felt lost without it. He wanted to run.

Sybil was his happiest thought. She became his life and he was fiercely jealous of her. It wasn't unusual to see Billy angry because she had been friendly with another boy. He would shout and storm; he even broke car windows with his fist a

couple of times. Sybil couldn't understand his consuming jealousy. Neither could Billy. But he had been robbed of his father's
love, and he would fight to the death anyone who might try to
move in on his only other love.

He found a little fun with the boys: a few beer busts on
weekends, a game of baseball, a hunting trip. He still enjoyed
reading, and he would even keep a novel going while in school
by hiding it behind a textbook. In spite of such diversions, he
was able to maintain good grades in his school work. Plains did
not offer much in the way of excitement for teen-age boys, and
one Saturday night Billy and a couple of buddies were scouring
the town looking for something to do. It showed a streak of
optimism that they even tried, but when they found none, they
decided to steal a couple of watermelons. They drove down the
dark highway toward our old home in the country, and just
before a sharp curve in the road, there was a car lane that
turned off to the right. Billy parked the car on the shoulder of
the lane, and one of his friends stayed to watch it as Billy and
the other boy made their way through a stand of sugar cane into
a field of watermelon. Each grabbed a large melon and headed
back to the car. They put the melons in the trunk, jumped in
the car laughing, and drove off into the night. An hour later,
the three melon thieves were stuffed and satisfied with their
petty theft.

The next morning at the breakfast table, Billy told Mother
about his escapade. "Where was that melon patch?" she asked.
"Behind the sugar cane field on the Haleses' road," Billy explained.

"I hate to tell you, Billy," Mother said with a tickled look
on her face, "but you stole those melons from yourself. That
patch belongs to us."

In April 1954, shortly after his seventeenth birthday, Billy
came down with a bad case of spring fever. There were all the

symptoms: daydreaming in the classroom; that antsy feeling that the big, wide, blooming world is going to waste; school is a drag; home is boring. The Columbus in him wanted to go discover America.

Walking out of the high-school entrance into the waiting warm afternoon, Billy turned to Wiley Booker, his tall, gangly sidekick, and one of his companions on the night of the watermelon caper. "Wiley, let's go to Miami!" Wiley gave him an "Aw-yer-kiddin' " look and then started to laugh. But he realized Billy was serious and crazy enough to do it. Wiley felt a surge of excitement. Miami! He had never been there. It took just two days from Billy's suggestion until he and Wiley had bankrolled their trip out of some of their mutual savings and were on the road, thumbing down Highway 280, through Americus, on to dusty, down-at-the-heels Valdosta, and across the border into Florida.

When they hit Dade County, the moss-laden oaks and palmetto of the Orange State flatland yielded to the silhouette of Miami. The long ride and sixteen different cars had dampened their wanderlust considerably until they saw those towering office buildings and apartments lining the Inland Waterway. They found a small park in Miami Beach and just people-watched for a while as they ate candy bars and downed Cokes. "Look at all the pretty women," Wiley said, ignoring the surrounding splendor. Billy just grinned and said nothing. He needed no encouragement from his observant buddy. It sure would be fun to have Sybil with me, he thought, but she wouldn't like us watching all these ladies.

After five days of swimming, sunburn, a diet of junk food, and a couple of expensive meals, they were ready to head home. They were broke and the nightly shoe-leather cruising of the streets and haunts of Miami hadn't come up with anything more exciting than meeting a couple of pretty girls from Jersey

City. That evolved into the foursome going to the Eden Roc for
a dinner the boys couldn't afford, and it ended by sitting in the
lobby with a polite "Thank you for a nice evening" from the
girls. That's not the way the story usually ends in the movies
but that was their finale.

Two days and several rides later, the intrepid pair were let
out at Bill Jennings's gas station in Plains, broke, weary, and
happy to be home. The old hometown looked mighty good. Of
course, they immediately began to weave stories of their exciting, worldly adventure. Their friends took it all in as Billy and
Wiley served them baloney sandwiched between fact, but it was
this catering of fact and fiction to their hungry buddies that
made the wild journey worthwhile.

Billy's oldest and dearest friend was, and still is, Bud Duvall.
They began the first grade together at Plains Grammar School,
and all the way through to graduation they shared their fun,
fishing, exploring, boy-talking. They fought a lot, too, but it
never lasted. They could be at each other's throats one day and
by the next day all was forgotten. Bud was the third culprit in
the watermelon caper, and it was a familiar sight to see him and
Billy whispering jests to each other outside Mr. Sheffield's office
as they waited for the principal to give them one of their frequent and ineffectual lectures on misconduct. A few times they
got the belt.

One of the things that deepened the bond between these two
is Bud's speech impediment. A lot of people can't understand
him, and it fell to Billy at an early age to be Bud's interpreter,
both to teachers and friends. Billy was needed most when Bud
got excited. Even as the two boys grew older, Billy was there
when a business transaction needed to be made in order to be
Bud's spokesman.

Bud shared memories with me recently while we stood to-

gether at Billy's gas station in Plains. This forty-year-old bachelor has been Billy's fiercely loyal buddy for more than thirty
years. And to Bud, Billy is just plain Billy.

"When we were just kids," Bud told me, "Billy and I used
to sell Cokes at the softball games every Sunday. We'd get a
dollar each for the whole day's work. Then later in high school,
Billy, Wiley Booker, and I would take up money to buy gas to
go to Americus to see a movie." Looking up at the gas pump
with a 62.9 cents posted for regular gas Bud said, "Back then
gas would be twenty-five cents a gallon. We could always scrape
up enough for two gallons. That'd get us over and back. We
usually went in the Carters' car. Billy would usually get to
borrow it. Of course, if Billy had a date with Sybil, he wouldn't
let us go.

"Billy owned his own fifty-three Model A later," Bud continued. "Hell of a car! We'd be pushing as much as driving.
There were some nights when I remember pushing it half a
mile, driving half a mile, pushing and driving all night. Hell of
a car! Thank God he got rid of it! Then he bought an old
Renault. Better car. Coming back from Americus one night it
got a flat tire. Billy found a nail that would fit in the hole, stuck
the nail in the hole, pumped up the tire, and drove to Plains.
Ain't that something? That ain't walkin' on water, but driving
home on a flat tire fixed with a nail is something else!"

The day after he graduated from high school, Billy drove the
thirty miles to Albany to join the Marine Corps in the company
of Bud, his pal through most of his school years. They were
driving the new Cadillac Mother had bought with the hope that
it might please Billy. She could sense that he was chaffing at the
bit, and she thought a new car would bring him a little of the
pleasure she couldn't. The two boys joked and laughed a lot as
they rode along—too much, the way people do to cover anxiety.
The June day was warm and humid. The dogwoods dappled the

woods with their delicate pinks and whites. But the car and the beauty of the day couldn't silence the cry of Billy's heart to get away from home. Like most of the older boys of the town, Billy had joined the National Guard so he wouldn't have to leave for the service, but he hated it. "Him and the Guard didn't get along so good," Bud said years later. As much as he feared leaving, Billy thought that joining the Marines was his only way out of the not-so-quiet desperation he was feeling. He had done well in high school. Billy would later claim that he graduated twenty-fifth in a class of twenty-six, but Sybil says that is just a self-demeaning fib. It used to upset her to see how little he had to study. "Then after all my hard study," she complains, "he would go into a test and get a good grade easily, and I had to work so hard."

A note to Billy from Miss Julia Coleman, his twelfth grade English teacher, attached to his final papers painted a different picture of him than he is wont to give. I don't remember the exact words of the note, but Miss Julia said that she had faith in Billy.

But Billy didn't believe in himself, and Mother sensed his mounting bitterness, his constant frustration. It wouldn't take much for him to chew her out or stalk out of the house. The pleasant, usually smiling young man was beginning to ask, "Who am I?" and "What's it all about?" All his bright mind could come up with was a troubling, "I don't know." Maybe "out there" he could put it together.

Six days after he had enlisted in the Marines, Billy sat with Sybil in Mother's car outside the rustic frame Pond House, the place our family retreated to on weekends. The next day he was leaving by train for Parris Island Boot Training Camp, and as they sat alone, Sybil buried her head in his encircling body and wept. "She cares that much," Billy thought. It quickened the man in this boy, and he said in comfort, "Sybil, as soon as I can

I'll come home and marry you like I promised. Then you can come and live with me where I'm stationed." The unusually mature fifteen-year-old girl he held in his arms was consoled but not deceived. She would marry him and follow him wherever he went because she loved him so, but she wanted him happy and she knew, without knowing what she knew, how deeply he hurt. She smiled up at him through her tears. There was nothing she could say. She knew he had to go, to keep looking for the Billy she had already found. She would do everything she could to help him find himself.

His formal proposal came later, on January 8, 1955, and it was typically Billy. Sitting with Sybil in the family car outside the football stadium at Georgia Southwest College, he made his unequivocal offer.

"Before we go into the ball game, Sybil," he said, "I've got something for you." He opened a little box, took out a ring and held it out to her.

"Oh, but, Billy," Sybil said, "I feel we're too young." She was fifteen and he was seventeen.

"Sybil," he replied, "age has nothing to do with it. You either love me or you don't."

"I do," she said. That was all he needed. He slipped the ring on Sybil's finger.

Both families were upset at the prospect of this teen-age marriage, but neither interfered. Mother called Dr. J. D. Martin, who had become our family physician after the death of Dr. Wise, seeking his advice. He had been one of the closest friends of the family for many years. "Lillian," he said, "Sybil may save Billy's life emotionally. She fills a big gap in that boy's life since Earl's death. Sybil is that important to Billy. Don't try to stop them."

Billy and Sybil were married on Sunday, August 21, 1955, the day after he graduated from boot camp.

He put on his dress uniform for the wedding, but he couldn't find the polished brass buckle, and he refused to go to the church without it. Mother called in everyone she could find to assist in the search. As time was running out, the buckle was found—under the sofa where Billy must have kicked it after cleaning it.

There, in the chancel of the Plains Baptist Church, Billy stood by the altar waiting for his bride to come down the aisle. He was tan and boot-camp trim. With his short hair, he looked so young. I saw Mother glance anxiously at him several times as though she couldn't quite believe her baby was about to be married. Her eyes began to glisten. Billy fairly glowed as Sybil, dressed in a white gown, joined him before the minister. After the brief ceremony, as they kissed, Mother's eyes overflowed.

Billy's gang had gone early to find and "fix" his car. By the time they finished, it was decked out in dangling beer cans and soap-scrawled graffiti. Then they waited to chase the newlyweds with horns blaring. From Plains all roads lead to Americus, but as Billy and Sybil left the Plains Baptist Church, they drove up the main highway and on to a side road leading to the cemetery. When the caravan saw where Billy was driving, the auto horns stopped sounding. The couple got out of the car and walked up to Daddy's grave. The pursuing wedding party looked on as Billy and Sybil placed her wedding bouquet on the grave marker. The couple stood for a moment with their heads bowed. Then they walked back to their car and drove off.

6

For Better or
for Worse

Their first few years of marriage were bumpy if not rocky. Sybil had never been away from home, and Billy was transferred to a camp near Chicago. Sybil stayed in Plains, planning to finish high school, but they missed each other too much. By the end of September, Billy couldn't stand the separation any longer and sent for her, and as soon as she could make all the necessary arrangements, an overjoyed Sybil headed for Chicago.

Mother took her to the train station to see her off, and immediately after the train pulled out, she called Billy in Chicago to give him Sybil's arrival time. Nervous and excited, Billy left early for the train station to be sure he was on time, but the country boy was shocked to find that there was more than one train station in Chicago, and he didn't know which station to go to. Furthermore, in his excitement, he forgot Sybil's arrival time, and when he called Mother to get the needed information, she was not at home. There was only one thing to do. Billy went from one station to the other looking for Sybil. He walked back and forth all night on foot because he had no car and too little money for a cab.

When Sybil arrived in Chicago, there was no one to meet her, and she was frightened. She called Billy's apartment, but no one answered, and finally began wandering aimlessly around the drab, dimly lighted station. Then as she looked down a row of benches, suddenly there he was—curled up on a bench asleep. Exhausted and frightened about the possible fate of his new bride, he had lain down and dozed off. "Billy, it's me, it's Sybil!" He lunged off the bench and stood there, confused for a moment. Then he shouted, "Sybil!" and took her in his arms.

Together they went to their little honeymoon castle, a one-room garage apartment. That first home was ever so humble with its "early matrimonial" boxes for cupboards and Goodwill Industry furniture. But Sybil was a good cook and housekeeper, and she felt very little homesickness. She liked her new life in the big city. She got a job in a dress shop, but her day really began when Billy opened the apartment door and walked in around six o'clock each evening.

Sybil, however, was soon to discover a Carter habit that other in-laws before her had found unbearable. While she got supper on the table, Billy read a book; when he sat in the tub, he read a book; when he went to bed, he took his book with him. Sybil suffered in silence. Her knight in shining armor was a book-worm in disguise. She tried to accept this flaw, but there was one thing she could not tolerate. When they came to the table for supper, that was the time to exchange comments on the day's events, catch up on news, and generally be together. To Sybil, reading at the table was intolerably rude and unloving. It didn't make any difference that Billy had done it all his life, and that Miss Lillian had permitted it, even encouraged it. Sybil expected mealtime to be her time with Billy.

One night she finally lost her patience. She had been especially lonely all day. The hours of waiting for Billy to come home had seemed endless. It was snowing outside, the first snow she had ever seen, and the weather was colder than she ever thought possible. She was sure she was pregnant because eating wasn't fun anymore. She even wondered if Billy loved her; the blues had really moved in. As Sybil awaited Billy's arrival, she said to herself, if he sits down at that table tonight and sticks a book up in front of my face, I'm leaving. I'm not putting up with it again.

Billy came in shaking the snow off his boots and coat. He took Sybil in his arms, gave her a kiss and a tight squeeze and then asked, "What's for supper?"

"Oh, it's your favorite. I've got fried chicken, mashed potatoes, butter beans, and biscuits."

"Well, good. I sure do want to light into that," Billy said as he began to strip off his damp clothes. Off came his shirt, undershirt, shoes and socks as he warmed his chilled body in front of an electric heater.

Sybil had gone to a lot of extra effort to make this supper as romantic as possible. A candle was burning in the center of the card table set for two. She lowered the lights and they sat down to eat. Then Billy did it. He picked up a book and began to squint at it in the candlelight. Sybil exploded.

"Good-bye forever!" she shouted. "I can't stand this any longer. You don't love me anymore."

Billy sat there stunned as Sybil put on her coat and walked out into the night, slamming the door behind her.

It was dark outside, darker than she had thought. And colder, too. The snowflakes mingled with the tears streaming down her cheeks. As the frigid air began to chill her, she started walking faster. Where she was going she didn't know, but it wasn't long before she knew she was lost. One street looked like another, and she stopped. Standing in the gently falling snow, she heard the crunching sound of footsteps behind her. Then the sound ceased. She took a few more steps and she heard the footsteps once again. Frightened, she began running. Someone was following her. She turned around to get a look at her pursuer but could see nothing in the darkness. Then she began to scream. "Who are you?"

"Sybil, it's me," a voice replied. It was Billy.

Sybil's panic was then replaced with anger again. "Billy Carter, I told you I never wanted to see you again."

"Sybil," he said, "I couldn't let you be out here alone. I'll stay far behind, but something could happen to you."

Sybil walked back toward Billy. When she was only a couple of feet from him she couldn't believe her eyes. "Billy, you don't have a shirt on," she said. "Crazy, you don't even have on any shoes or socks. You'll catch your death of cold."

Billy held out his chilled arms and she ran into his embrace. Arm in arm, they walked back to their apartment, and Sybil knew as never before how much he loved her.

Many times since, Sybil has eaten with Billy's face buried in a book. She confesses that she gets discouraged about it, but then she remembers that walk in the snow, and she has long accepted this bad habit as a part of Billy. There are still times, though, when she can't stand the book. When that happens she is not above reaching over, plucking the book out of Billy's hands, and throwing it as far as she can. Billy won't pick it up until after dinner. Most people learn how to read. Sybil is still trying to teach Billy how *not* to read.

A few weeks after their walk in the snow, Billy again proved to Sybil that he cared. A Marine Corps buddy came to him in financial distress; he had lost his paycheck gambling and had failed to send any money to his mother, who was dependent on him. "Billy," he pleaded, "I'll pay you back, but I've got to get some money to my mother right away and I lost all mine in a crap game." Billy took out his wallet and gave him every penny he had.

To his chagrin, he arrived home that Friday evening to find that Sybil hadn't been able to buy groceries because he had forgotten to leave her any money. Counting all their coins, they discovered they had twenty-five cents between them and payday wasn't until Monday afternoon. Sybil had to have bus fare to get to her job on Monday morning or have a long, cold walk. Billy's shortsighted generosity left them broke. Sybil just laughed. That's Billy, she thought. Now the big decision was, how would they spend their twenty-five cents—on food or fare?

"Sybil," Billy decided, "it'll be for your bus fare to work." "No," Sybil protested, "I'll walk and we'll get a loaf of bread. We have a little butter and jelly."

But Billy was determined. He wasn't going to let her suffer for his stupidity. "We're not going to starve," he said, "and you're not going to walk." And his woman didn't walk.

After a year and two months in Chicago, Billy received orders to go to Japan, and the young couple faced their first lengthy separation. Sybil went home to live with her parents until Billy returned to the United States.

Six months after he began his overseas tour of duty, his first child, daughter Kim, was born. In their separation Sybil lived with her mother in Plains. They have always been very close. Lucille spent much of her time helping Sybil with her new baby. Sybil, in turn, helped her freeze vegetables and can fruits and jellies. After Billy's return, he was stationed at Parris Island, North Carolina. There, Sybil gave birth to their second child, Jana Kae.

During his four years in the Marines, Billy traveled, courtesy of the Corps, to Japan, Okinawa, and several other Asian countries. He didn't do any fighting with foreign troops, but he did get into a few battles.

"At that point," he recalls, "I just thought I was a tough old boy ready to raise hell. I started out trying to whip five sailors at once and losing. Then I lost some one-on-one fights. I quit fighting after the biggest one of my Marine career, in an enlisted men's club in Japan. Ten of us Southern boys were trying to get rid of a honky-tonk record and play hillbilly music. By the time the argument was settled, there was one broken record and damn near ten dead hillbillies."

After his discharge from the Marines in 1959, Billy returned to Sybil and his two daughters in Plains and went to work for Jimmy. His job was driving the fertilizer truck and doing odd jobs assigned by Jimmy, and the predictable pressures began to mount. He couldn't stand to be a hired hand in the business he had thought would be his. He felt frustrated and bitterly un-happy—with himself, with Jimmy, with his job, and with just about everything. Billy had always liked beer, but now his nightly consumption went up by a few cans.

Buddy, their third child, was born not long after he returned to Plains, and the birth of Billy's first son was perhaps the happiest moment during the brief time he tried to find a place for himself in his hometown.

When Sybil went into labor, Billy took her to the hospital, and he was there cheering her on every minute. As soon as his son was born, Billy ran to the phone to call Mother. He was so excited he could only stutter. The more Mother questioned him about the birth, the more excited he became.

"What is it, Billy?" Mother asked. "Has Sybil had the baby?"

"Y-y-y-y-y-yes, M-m-m-m-mom," he stuttered.

"What is it?" she asked again.

"Ma-ma-ma-ma." No words would form.

"Is Sybil all right? Is the baby all right?"

"Ma-ma-ma-ma-ma."

"Is it a girl?"

"Ma-ma-ma-ma-ma-ma-ma."

"Is it a boy?"

"Mama, it's a b-b-boy!" Billy screamed.

It was a boy, and Billy was in seventh heaven. He wanted to take him home on the first day. Every day after that he asked again if he could take his boy home. It was six days before the doctor consented.

Usually Billy felt someone else was better at getting Sybil and the new baby home from the hospital because he felt so clumsy, but this time he went to the hospital to pick up mother and baby alone—and on time. He went up to Sybil's room and helped tie a little bonnet on the baby's head, and then he carefully wrapped him in a yellow blanket. The nurse helped Sybil down the hospital steps and out to the car while Billy carried the baby. When they arrived home, he pulled the car up as close to the door as possible and came around to Sybil's side. He opened the door, tenderly lifted the baby out of her arms, and like a conquering hero, he carried his son into the house. Sybil waited for him to return to help her. She waited and waited. About half an hour later she managed *slowly* to open the door and ease out of the car. Carefully she made her way up the steps into the house, and when she walked into the baby's room, she saw Billy sitting in the middle of the floor, lost in conversation with his son. It was the beginning of a love relationship which has grown through the years.

After a year and a half of homecoming malaise, Billy quit his job at the warehouse and moved Sybil and his three children to Atlanta, where he enrolled in Emory University. He thought a college education would help him find what he should do in life, but he hated college from the beginning. He couldn't stand being cooped up in a classroom and he had little motivation for the highly competitive academic atmosphere he found there. Marle, their fourth child and third daughter, was born during the year Billy and Sybil spent in Atlanta. But soon after her birth, Billy quit Emory and moved his family to Macon, Georgia.

The time spent in Macon was the lowest period of Billy's life. Getting older, he had a growing sense of no purpose or direction. During this stressful period, Sybil had two miscarriages, and what once had been small spats now became those angry fights made of one part authentic gripe and nine parts broken heart.

Billy worked at a succession of jobs, including construction labor and selling paint, but they were just jobs, putting in time. He was now experiencing a sense of total failure, and he tried to drown his agony in beer. Night after night, Sybil would walk into their dingy little living room after putting the children to bed only to find the man she adored with his tenth can of beer in his hand staring into space. His drinking was out of control, and Billy couldn't shake the feeling that his dream of running the business and farms in Plains had been a cruel hoax. There seemed to be no hope of realizing his lifelong ambition, and he had run out of alternatives. Billy felt he could never work for anyone other than his father and there was no way he wanted to return to his hometown except as part of his father's business. He was bitterly frustrated.

Meanwhile back in Plains, Jimmy was deep into the job of running the warehouse and the family farms. He had studied agriculture and the fine points of everything from crop rotation to seed culture. He investigated the newest methods of ginning cotton and drying, shelling, and cleaning peanuts. He loved the challenge, and the business was growing through his administrative skill. It is one of life's ironies that Jimmy, who never wanted the peanut business and dreamed of the sea, found it his, while Billy, who never wanted anything else, was denied it—and thought he always would be.

Part II
Coming Home

*We all sat silently in front of a television set in Jimmy's room
at the Americana Hotel in New York as the program switched
over to Madison Square Garden. The National Anthem was
being played as the convention opened, and the balloting for the
presidential nominee of the Democratic party would soon begin.*

*Jimmy stood up. With a pensive look he slowly walked across
the room. He stopped and spoke with quiet, brooding emotion.
"One phase of my life is coming to a close tonight and a new
phase is beginning." It was as if he didn't want to move into that
awesome new chapter alone. He seemed to be saying, "Share this
moment with me, please." I had never seen Jimmy look like he
did at that moment. Or maybe I was just seeing more clearly the
strength, the power of this man's soul. He let out an audible sigh.
He then focused his gaze on the one who most deeply would have
to share it all, every victory, every defeat—Rosalynn. "It's okay
now," he said. "You can go."*

*Only Mother remained behind with Jimmy. Rosalynn, Billy,
and I, along with other members of our family, went to Madison
Square Garden. Just as we took our seats, Congressman Peter*

77

Rodino, who had chaired the House of Representatives probe of the Watergate scandal, rose to make the first nomination speech. Jimmy had won the poll position by the luck of the draw that afternoon. "With honest talk and plain talk," said Rodino, "Jimmy Carter has appealed to the American people. . . ." He concluded his speech by declaring that Jimmy was the only man who could unite the Democratic party and our nation and bring America "back to a position of respect and esteem in the eyes of the world."

Other nominations followed—Ellen McCormack, the anti-abortion candidate, and Congressman Morris Udall. Using his right to second his own nomination, Udall actually spoke in support of Jimmy. "This is a good man," he said. "When he says he'll beat you, he beats you fair and square."

When the delegate count got underway, it went pretty much as Jimmy's convention experts had predicted. Alabama began. It cast thirty votes for Jimmy and five votes for George Wallace. The alphabetical roll call of states continued—Alaska, California, Massachusetts, Missouri, New Hampshire. The count for Jimmy slowly increased. After New Hampshire it was at the 1,025½ mark. New Jersey was next. Finally at 11:11 P.M., Ohio cast all 132 of its delegate votes for Jimmy. He was over the top.

Jimmy had won the nomination.

Suddenly the auditorium echoed with cheers. We were engulfed in pandemonium. All the Carters were acting slightly delirious. I was expressing excitement, but inside I felt numb. The whole convention now seemed to be choreographed bedlam. One can stand only so much excitement, and I had overloaded. I felt no real thrill, just a deep sense of relief that, at last, he had won. I was almost overcome with a feeling of disbelief bordering on unreality. So, when I looked over at Billy and he had a get-me-out-of-here expression on his face, I understood. The roll call continued. But the delegates knew it was all over. Someone had scrawled a homemade banner which read, "We Love You, Billy." Two delegates were lifting it aloft and parading it on the floor below the family section. Billy responded with a shy smile. I don't think he will ever feel totally comfortable with his celebrity status.

As quickly as possible, after the roll call of the state delegations was over, the Secret Service shepherded the family out of the Garden and into a waiting bus. Back at the Americana, we went directly up to the twenty-first floor. The Secret Service agents guarding Jimmy's suite had memorized the faces of the family by the end of the first day, so there was no delay. An agent opened the door, and we entered the ornate living room with its mint green velveteen drapes and plush matching Karistan carpet. Jimmy greeted each of us with a warm embrace and that light-up-the-world smile of his.

We all stood around him in a loose semicircle. A few minutes after we arrived, Jimmy's closest associates filed in: Hamilton Jordan, Jerry Rafshoon, and Jody Powell. There was a flood of excited conversation. All of us abandoned deference. We were trying to express our love and gratitude! "You made it, Jimmy!" "Oh, Rosalynn, we're so proud of both of you!" "We love you!" The excited sharing continued to pour out until Jimmy motioned and said he wanted to speak to everyone. The room fell silent.

"You know how much I love all of you," he began. "You know how much I appreciate all you have done for me. But the one person I feel most grateful to, the one I feel did the most to make it possible for me to wage this campaign and to make this night of victory possible . . ." he turned to the man standing to his right, "is my brother, Billy."

Looking directly at him, Jimmy said, "Billy, I want to thank you. Without you, it couldn't have happened. You stayed home and kept everything going." He couldn't say anything more. They went into each other's arms.

7

A Dream
Come True

The path to that moment on the night of Jimmy's nomination had been precipitous and painful.

In May 1963, Jimmy knew he had exhausted the challenge of the family business. The peanut warehouse, which had grossed $187 the first year he ran it, was now grossing over two million dollars annually. Jimmy was interested in politics, and he had his eye on a seat in the Georgia senate. But running for state public office would demand more time than he could give it if he was still operating the business. A review of possible successors took only a minute. There was only one person for the job. And that was Billy.

Jimmy drove over to Macon to see Billy. When Sybil opened the door of their little gray house with peeling asphalt shingles and saw her brother-in-law, she felt apprehensive. What is Jimmy doing here? she thought. They greeted each other almost formally. Billy heard his brother's voice and came out of the back bedroom as his children warmly greeted their uncle.

When Jimmy saw his brother he felt a tug on his heart. Billy always reminded him of his father. His appearance and mannerisms were very much like Earl Carter's.

Jimmy didn't even wait to sit down. "Billy," he said directly, "I've come to ask you to manage the business." He then laid out his plan to run for the state senate.

Billy was sick of his job at the paint store, and although it still galled him to think of working for his brother, Jimmy's request was the most hopeful thing to come along since he got out of the Marines. He looked at Sybil. She had put up with a lot during his drifting and serious drinking. She rarely criticized her man, but they had come close to divorce when oceans of beer began to separate them.

That was two years ago. Fortunately, a friend of Billy's saw his problem and told him one day at the paint store that he had heard about an Alcoholics Anonymous group in Albany that he might find helpful. It met every Thursday night. "I understand from a guy I work with," the friend said, "that it helps you take a look at life and get a hold of yourself. He said it helped him a lot."

Suspicious of anyone who got more personal than a friendly bartender, Billy went to the meeting the next week, but he kept his guard up. The whole night he didn't say a word except to fend off every question but "What is your name?" He answered that. He sat looking at the other members of the group, wondering why he did such a stupid thing as to come in the first place. But after he heard a couple of them describe feelings that were just like what he had been feeling, and how they were dealing with their stress, Billy decided to return.

He never did know whether his brief three-month association with the group gave him much new insight, or whether it was just being able to talk with people who were honest enough to say they were hurting, but the group helped Billy get away from the hopeless feeling he had carried around for five years. And he lightened up on his drinking.

Now Billy was ready to make another positive step in his life, and there was only one answer he could give to Jimmy's request to return to Plains and manage the family business. "I'd like to give it a try," he said in a barely audible response.

Billy, Sybil, and the children moved back to Plains into the old wood-frame house which, with major alterations, would be their home for the next twelve years.

With Billy's return, Jimmy put his political plans into action, and as he spent more days on the road, Billy took on more of the business responsibilities. It felt good to be in the saddle he had wanted to be in for so long. Rosalynn was still the book-keeper, and at times she and Billy clashed over business matters. But usually they worked together harmoniously. When Jimmy came home for a few days, he and his brother would take long walks in the fields. They had little common ground in religion, beer, or politics, so they talked mainly about business. Jimmy remembers those walks as the time when he came to know his much younger brother for the first time. He had gone off to college when Billy was still a baby. Now he was getting to know him man to man. Billy salted a lot of their conversations with his homespun humor. Some of the farmers and workers still recall the two brothers trudging through fields together, filling them with laughter.

Jimmy reached his first political milestone in 1964, when he was elected to the Georgia state senate. It was a hard fight. The election was preceded by a brutal campaign in which his opponent was guilty of voter fraud. Jimmy proved in court, with the aid of Atlanta attorney Charlie Kirbo, that the ballots in one election district had been falsely cast in large enough numbers to decide the election against him. Circuit judge George Crowe was appalled by the blatant corruption, and declared Jimmy the winner. There were further political machinations by his opponent, but Jimmy prevailed. And he was on the road which would ultimately lead to the White House.

That same year, Billy passed a milestone of his own: He bought a one-sixth share in the warehouse. The night he was invited to buy in, he came home to Sybil to tell her the good news. She was at the sink cleaning some vegetables, and when the door opened she called out, "Billy, is that you?" She turned around. He was standing at the kitchen door, smiling puckishly. He was doing a poor job of looking nonchalant.

"Jimmy offered me a sixth of the business," he said, still smiling.

"Oh, Billy!" Sybil said, as she threw her arms around him. More than anyone on earth, she knew what this meant to him. He was no longer working for his brother. He was his partner.

But for Billy the satisfaction went much deeper than that. He was walking a little taller with his own share of his father's creation. "Buckshot," Daddy once told him, "one day this business is going to be yours to run." Something inside Billy said that night, "I made it, Daddy."

8

Giving Plains
the Business

Billy works hard, plays hard, and loves hard; and as he began
to reestablish himself in Plains, he started building three worlds
where he could give expression to each of these parts of the
emerging Billy Carter.

From six A.M. to five P.M. he gave his total attention to the
warehouse. And during the harvest season he was there almost
twenty-four hours a day, sometimes grabbing a catnap in the
office and then returning to scores of details that needed attention: machinery maintenance and repair, weighing, grading,
storing, supply requisition, shipping, bookkeeping, government
inspection, safety requirements, to name only a few. He was
proving to be a first-class businessman. Billy wasn't the techno-
crat his brother was, but he had a great way with the farmers.
They respected and trusted him. Plus, he seemed to be more
their kind of people than his older brother. This, it appears, was
a key factor in the business growth under his management.

After hours a different Billy expressed himself. He tried never
to bring the business home with him. When he was with the
family he focused all his attention on them. With little children
to take care of, Sybil and Billy usually kept close to home. But

sometimes they were able to leave them with their grandmother and take short trips to Atlanta or go see a ball game. Sometimes they would just hop in the car and drive over the farms with the children in the back seat. His home was very important to him, and Sybil was still his best friend.

Then there came the times when he enjoyed jumping into his pickup and rendezvousing with the close circle of buddies which had formed since he came home. Their frequent watering hole was Joe's, a beer joint and gas station located about two miles outside of Plains. One of the favorite moments to remember among the boys took place at Joe's on the last day of harvest in 1964. Billy and his buddies were joined by a crowd of farmers and field hands who wanted to celebrate the end of their big push to get the final load of peanuts in. There was a sameness about their fatigued faces covered with dust and grime. Their heavy brogans were caked with red clay, and their overalls and billed caps were streaked and spotted with the same red South Georgia soil. Joe, the proprietor, had barbecued a pig for the occasion. Peanuts were boiling in a large cast-iron pot heating over an open fire in the field beside the station. Beer and laughter were in evidence everywhere.

As the festivities got into high gear, Billy in a burst of manic delight, jumped up on the roof of his car, which was parked near the cluster of celebrants, and began to twirl his billed cap on his finger—once, twice, a third time. Then he flung it into the fire shouting, "To hell with all the troubles of the world!" Suddenly everyone was removing his hat, twirling it three times and throwing it in the fire to a chorus of shouts: "To hell with all the troubles of the world." The scene of grown men turned carefree boys, laughing and shouting while burning their favorite work hats, was so exhilarating to everyone there that it was destined to be an annual harvest-end event, and a ceremony was born.

Outside of Plains that ritual may only excite the hat merchants of the world. But it is an annual affair cherished by those select few who are allowed to participate in it.

In 1970, Billy heard that Mill Jennings's Amoco station was up for sale. He bought it for $10,000, and his reasons for the purchase were more social than economic. The place was run-down (and still is). Under the faded second or third coat of paint, the former owner's name can still be distinguished: it barely reads, " EN INGS." The station pumped only a few hundred gallons of gas a month; the old man's ledger showed a small profit for the sale of oil, tires, batteries, and a few lube jobs. But all totaled, it made a sum slightly higher than the monthly electric bill. That didn't really matter. Billy wanted the station as a home for his down-home fraternity.

Soon after Billy took over, he cleared a place in the storage room and added some cast-off furniture, featuring a tattered overstuffed chair and a recycled truck seat which acted as a sofa. It was their new clubhouse, and when Billy and his friends first settled in, the Coke cooler was always filled with beer. It was understood that any of the group could help himself and then leave a donation. That eliminated any problems with authorities about selling beer without a license. But not long after he acquired the Amoco station, Billy applied for a state permit to sell beer on the premises. When the application was approved, it was the scandal of that predominantly dry Baptist town.

Mother was a member of a "stitch and chat" group which met each week, and she knew all the women would be furious over this breach of Baptist morals. She wasn't looking forward to facing a roomful of piqued questioners at the next meeting. So Mother decided to try to smooth things over. She had Billy prepare some statistics for her before going to the meeting.

Mother arrived at the hostess's house a little late, and everyone was stiffly polite as she took her chair. But no one uttered a word. Then with all the calm she could muster, Mother said, "Have you heard that Billy has bought Mill Jennings's station?"

A few nodded.

"And did you know he got two beer licenses? One so that the beer could be carried off the premises and one so it could be drunk there."

Nods again.

"And did you know that in the first week he sold twenty-two cases of beer with a five cent tax on each can which goes into the Plains treasury? That means that Billy's beer sales will probably put more dollars into the Plains treasury than all the people in Plains will pay in taxes in a year put together. Isn't that wonderful?"

Mother's diplomacy was successful. Honesty is always the best policy, and now all the facts were out in the open. The conversation changed and Billy's beer license was never mentioned again until the unspoken undercurrent of disapproval surfaced years later when he ran for mayor.

None of this flap caused much of a stir in the back room of the Amoco station. Bud Duvall, a very shy, quiet, kind man, kidded Billy about turning Plains into one great, big saloon, and they all had a good laugh. None of the boys could understand what the fuss was all about. They didn't want to corrupt anyone's morals. They just wanted their little oil-spotted oasis. Now they had it and loved it.

Billy enjoyed playing host to the gathered clan each afternoon. The tough, shrewd businessman who during working hours wouldn't give four sentences to a nonessential visitor shed the cloak of responsibility from his fleshy 5'6" frame and became a lighthearted, jesting, seldom serious, one-of-the-boys. The atmosphere was always casual. It was a come-as-you-are gathering. That usually meant work clothes—overalls or denim

coveralls—and the most common head gear was billed caps
with "Standard Oil" embroidered across the front.

The regulars never excluded visitors. Anyone who wandered
into the cluttered frame structure was welcome to share the pub
that friendship and thirst built. During the summer of 1976,
when Jimmy was campaigning for the presidency, it wasn't
unusual to see one of the local Carter gang wearing an ABC
television cap, or some other company hat one of them had
conned off a reporter or a cameraman.

The world discovered how much Billy thought of his gas
station in that same summer. It was a humid, sweltering August
day, and the usual weekend softball game was going on between
the local businessmen and the Secret Service men who were
assigned to protect Jimmy and his family during the campaign.
Billy was the pitcher for one team and Jimmy for the other. The
game was being played on a field not far from the station, and
Billy's team was ahead, 6–2, when all of a sudden there was a
loud explosion and billows of dark smoke began to pour out of
the station.

"My God, my station is burning down!" Billy screamed as
he raced toward the fire. A photographer stood there calmly
snapping pictures of the burning building. Billy flared. "Does
everything have to be a story, a news event?" He headed for the
cameraman with his fists clenched, but a couple of his friends
grabbed him and restrained him.

As Billy stood there watching smoke pouring out of his
beloved station, he broke into tears and said, "It's all I've got."
But he quickly regained his composure and sense of humor. "It
all started," he jested, "when the governor was losing the ball
game. Y'all set the service station on fire just so we wouldn't
win a game."

What had really happened was that a teen-ager put a coin in
the Coke machine. The cooler shorted out and sparks flew from

it, igniting fumes from a parked gasoline truck. The explosion that followed blew out one wall. Two young men were hospitalized with second- and third-degree burns.

Billy's cry, "It's all I've got" didn't seem to be a very sensible statement since he was the manager and part owner of a thriving peanut warehouse business. But in his heart the warehouse was still Jimmy's and Mother's. The Amoco station was all his.

Recently, Bud Duvall sat outside on the bench in front of Billy's station with some of the men in the town. It was a crisp Sunday morning, freshly laundered by a spring rain. Billy wasn't there. The men started to reminisce about the old days, and Bud began reflecting on his old friend.

"Yeah, he's got a quick mind, Billy does—a two-track mind. You can be talking to him when he's reading a book and he repeats back everything you've said—and he never slows up reading that book. He was the same way in school. He would be reading a book in class that had nothing to do with the lesson. The teacher would see him reading and ask him a question about what she had been saying. Billy, he'd look up, answer the question, and go back to the book and keep on reading. Buddy, his son, is the same way."

Bud also reflected on Billy's generosity. "I remember the day Billy bought this station," he said. "He found me and gave me the key and he said, 'Bud, anytime you want or need anything, just go in and get it.' How many people would give you the key to the business and never question what you got or if you paid for it? Sometimes I don't pay anything for a long time. Then I'll go in and put the money in the cash register—everything I owe. He never knows when I come or go. When Billy trusts somebody, you can have anything he's got. But if Billy doesn't trust you, he isn't going to give that person the time of day."

Warming to the subject of their unswerving loyalty to each other, Bud said solemnly, with a hand-on-the-Bible absoluteness, "Billy will never let me down, and I won't ever let him down."

"How about the rest of the family?" someone asked.

"I feel close to them," Bud answered. "Billy's children call me or stop by my house every day to see if I need anything. They want to know if I've picked up my mail yet. Sometimes they get me groceries. They are mighty thoughtful kids. They call me Mr. Bud. I feel close to the whole family. You don't find many friends like that.

"Miss Lillian," he said, "treats me like part of the family. She gets on me like she gets on Billy. Loves me like she loves him," he added with great pride, "but she really chews me out good when I need it."

That kind of cracker-barrel sharing is a real part of the Amoco station legend. But Bud's reflections on his friend's devotion to him and his closeness to Billy's family are a commentary on that third world in which Billy lived. Those whom he loved, especially his wife and kids, had become his most important asset. His small circle of loyal friends were only slightly less important to him. As Bud indicated, Billy would never deliberately let them down. Success and prominence would test this commitment, but it would not destroy it.

9

Like the Girl
with the Curl

The greatest sacrifice Jimmy had to make as Georgia state
senator was the frequent absence from his family which the
office required. In a speech years later he spoke of the domestic
price he paid. Jackie and Chip, his two older sons, were teen-
agers when Jimmy became state senator Carter, and both boys
hold their Uncle Billy in grateful memory for being their surrogate father during those high school years. Billy employed them
part time at the warehouse, doing the same odd jobs he did
before and after his father died and left him, and there were
many times when he took time out to talk to the boys father
to son. They remember how he bailed them out of some tough
teen-age jams. He never condemned them, but he did level with
them when he saw they were in danger of hurting themselves
or others. And more frequently they would seek him out. When
no one would listen or understand, they knew Uncle Billy
would.

His relationship with his own children is marked by the same
commendable devotion. But his attitude toward Sybil, his wife,
is an unbelievable mixture of insane jealousy, male chauvinism,
and almost religious dedication.

One New Year's Eve, Billy took Sybil to a dance in Americus. It was a pleasant enough evening with the standard gaudy trappings of confetti, streamers, balloons, and too much champagne. Then about an hour before the New Year, a stranger came up and asked Sybil for a dance. It had to be a stranger. Anybody who knew Billy knew that he was insanely jealous of her. He went out on the dance floor and asked the intruder what he thought he was doing taking his wife away from him. Before cooler or more sober heads could prevail, fists were swinging, bottles and glasses smashing, people scattering as two angry bucks had it out. The fight went wildly, inconclusively on until the police broke it up. The place was in shambles. Billy's bill for damage to the night spot was something shy of five thousand dollars, but he had made his point: No man's lovin' arms are going to hold Sybil but his.

That may be old-fashioned, even bull-headed, but that's Billy. When it comes to Sybil he is totally possessive. He would never cheat on her, but that is only symptomatic of something much more basic. Here is a man who had the first most important love of his life wrested from him when his father died. Sybil is the one who not only brought him the beauty and warmth of a very lovely, unusually stable woman's affection, she became the secure parental love he lost when Earl Carter was taken from him. That is why Billy would rather fight than share any part of her.

The whole wild New Year's Eve disaster left Sybil confused and angry. "I couldn't understand," she said later. "There are so many emotions he has that I've never been able to understand. Billy's got such a different nature." Sybil is predictable, calming, mature; Billy is mercurial, intense, volcanic. If he is the turbulent, boisterous, exhilarating wind in the sail of the ship of their life, she is the keel.

After over twenty years of marriage to Billy, Sybil confesses she still can't understand him. "I learn something new about him almost every day," she admits. "It's exciting! It's never boring living with him. But he can wear you absolutely to a frazzle. He has so many emotions; he has so many thoughts. His mind clicks so fast. It's impossible to stay up with him, much less ever get a step ahead. Sometimes I thank God I have no Carter blood in me, but I'm not sorry I married one."

Carter blood—hot, frigid, murky, radiant, mystical, practical, driving—oh, how driving—Carter blood. Adulthood sent the Carter children in four different directions—all passionately wanting to find fulfillment and wanting to achieve, as if every corpuscle in our veins wanted to be the best. Jimmy says that Admiral Hyman Rickover challenged him to eschew anything but the best. And that may be the case. But there is a will to excellence in all the Carter kids. It is what makes us anything but boring, sometimes wonderful, sometimes unbearable, and always incorrigible overachievers.

As Billy was working to be the best businessman, redneck, and beer drinker Plains ever saw, his sister Gloria was not exactly settling down to a life of average domesticity. After a brief and unhappy first marriage, she returned to Plains, and in 1949, met and married Walter Spann. He was then just beginning to develop his peanut farm, buying new land and implements, and the farm and his contract harvesting business have since made him a millionaire. Gloria is an accomplished artist and a sensitive poet who loves cross-country trips with Walter on their Harley-Davidson motorcycles.

She had a deep religious experience after she returned to Plains. Her eloquent and inspiring sharing of it with friends led to invitations as a conference speaker six years before I received my first invitation to speak. She enjoyed the opportunity, but after two years of growing demand for her ministry, she knew that this particular expression of her faith was not for her. She continued riding her big bike, and sometimes even found herself in the role of den mother to a bunch of motorcycle gang members. She did it her way.

As Jimmy advanced into the political major league, Gloria threw herself into his campaign for governor of Georgia. She managed the office in Plains almost singlehandedly, answering the phone, typing letters, stuffing envelopes, and recording every donation. In other words, she was the Jimmy Carter for Governor office in his hometown. She wasn't too interested in Billy's activities. They would exchange infrequent phone calls and she was grateful for his new beginning as warehouse manager. But their interests were too widely separated to sustain any close tie.

I have always felt close to Billy, closer to him than to Jimmy or Gloria, in spite of our differences in temperament and lifestyle. I was always a little in awe of Jimmy. I was still in elementary school when he left home to go to college, and the greatest thrill of my teen years was when he returned as a Naval Academy midshipman and took me on a date to Atlanta. We went to a nice restaurant, where I had my first sip of champagne, and then we saw a nightclub show. I don't recall what it was. It wasn't the culture; it was the company that made the evening so memorable. I felt cheated when Jimmy later married my best friend, Rosalynn. My idolized brother and my dearest friend lost to matrimony.

As an adult I see great depth in Gloria, an admirable will to be herself. But in my formative years, we felt an intense sibling rivalry and always kept a protective distance between us. I blame myself for not seeing earlier her unique beauty.

Billy, on the other hand, has always been my baby brother. I find him easy to love. He is vulnerable and human. I see his immense flaws, but I also see his strengths and potential. I believe in him. When he took over the reins of the business, I was sure he would succeed. It came as no surprise to me that he did so well as the entrepreneur of the Carter warehouse or that he is such a caring husband and father.

At nineteen, still recoiling from the unprotected world into which I walked when I left my home for college, I decided to leave Georgia State College for Women to marry a young veterinarian by the name of Bobby Stapleton. My father, knowing how dependent I was on him, advised his new son-in-law to move his practice away from Plains. We settled in North Carolina. On our last night before leaving home, I wept for hours. I felt that separation from my father, from Plains, and all that I knew was a death I couldn't bear.

During the first twelve years of my marriage, I was busy raising four children. It was an emotionally difficult time for me. I was a member of six different civic and special interest clubs at one time. I know now that all that activity was my way of trying to run from the unhappiness within myself and my home life. This period of my life saw a decline in my contact with Billy.

All the Carter children had gone their separate ways until we came together again to campaign for Jimmy in 1964. While Billy tended the store and Gloria ran the campaign office, I spent every available day on the campaign trail in Georgia, concentrating my efforts in Atlanta. Every Sunday night I boarded the train out of Fayetteville to Atlanta, and by midmorning I was in the streets handing out brochures and approaching people in shopping malls with "I'm Jimmy Carter's sister. Please vote for him for governor." It was hard work, and sometimes humiliating when someone favoring Lester Maddox, the segregationist candidate in the Democratic primary, verbally attacked me. Once a woman swung her purse at me, striking me across the face. In a couple of such nasty moments, I dissolved in tears and walked away.

It was a shock when Jimmy lost the primary race. The fact
that he was called "Jimmy who?" meant nothing to me. I knew
Jimmy and I knew he was a winner. The night of his primary
defeat to Maddox, who had none of Jimmy's leadership qualities or stature, was when I lost my political innocence. I was
angry and disillusioned. I had watched my brother work night
and day to win. He was down to 130 pounds and physically ill
on the day of his defeat. He was the better candidate by far and
yet the people didn't want him.

I returned to Fayetteville to take up the Christian service
which had come out of a recent spiritual awakening. I was
grateful for the meaning and love I had discovered in Jesus
Christ. I had no idea at that time that Jimmy would have a
similar spiritual renewal and that it would give him the confi-
dence and courage to do the impossible. With less than a week
of rest and recuperation after his primary defeat, he began to
work with total concentration and intensity on his campaign to
win the next election for governor in 1970.

Billy's interest in state and national politics began long before
Jimmy's involvement. He was never reluctant to express his
political views. Yet he was quite happy to keep the peanut
business healthy and growing, care for his family, and enjoy his
beer-irrigated social life. But as Jimmy's campaign activities
started into high gear again, they often intruded on his younger
brother. Billy has a way of taking such invasions of his privacy
for just so long and then, stand back. There will be an explosion.

One Saturday afternoon he was reading a good book and
polishing off a Carlings Black Label. (He switched to Pabst later
because he liked their delivery truck driver better. How's that
for taste in beer?) The telephone rang. Billy answered it. Business. It rang again. Jimmy's political business. Again it jangled.
More political business. He couldn't relax. It was hopeless to
try to read with continual interruptions. So Billy decided, "If

that damn phone rings one more time, I'm going to do something about it."

Rrrrrrrrriiiiiiiinnnnnnnggggggg!

Rrrrrrrrriiiiiiiinnnnnnnngggg!

That did it! In resolute fury, Billy walked to the phone, reached down and took the cord in his hand and gave it one powerful jerk. The wires separated from the wall. He then picked up the phone, carried it to the front door, walked out on the porch, and threw it as far as the monster would go.

Several neighbors saw the phone lying out in the yard and graciously carried it up to the front door intending to return it. Whichever member of the family answered the door asked the puzzled neighbors if they would please return it to where they found it. The phone lay out on the lawn for several weeks. When Billy was satisfied that the little black monster wasn't going to strangle him to death, he retrieved it and informed the family that he was calling the phone company to revive it.

While Billy may be a political agnostic, there have been moments when he made unintended but positive contributions to Jimmy's political career just by being a caring person. One Sunday he pulled his car off the road behind a vehicle that had broken down at the Plains city limits. The stranded driver was peering under the hood, and a worried woman and an elderly lady were seated inside.

"What's the trouble?" Billy asked.

"I don't know," the man said. "The old car stalled on me and I can't get it started. Anywhere in town I can get a mechanic to look at it?"

"It's Saturday," Billy replied, "everything's closed."

"Where's the nearest town?" The man was beginning to get upset.

"It's Americus, but everything's closed there, too. Where are you headed?"

"To Florida. I'm taking my mother-in-law home."

"Well," Billy said, "you take my car."

Taken aback by the offer, the man said, "But I don't even know you."

"Well, my car's better than yours. I'd be the loser if I never saw you again."

"But you don't know me. Why are you doing this?"

"Because you have to get your mother-in-law home."

A very surprised and grateful stranger found himself, as soon as he dropped Billy off at home, driving to Florida in Billy's car.

There have been times, however, when Billy was thoughtless, like the well-publicized "nigger" gaffe. In the summer of 1977, the press and television made a lot of a comment said in jest to an Oakland, California, politician named Carter Gilmore, a black who was running on the slogan, "Let's elect another Carter." At a party Gilmore prodded Billy with joking questions about the possibility that they might be distantly related. Billy couldn't resist the temptation to rib him in return. "I hate to say this," he finally answered, "but we've all left a nigger in the woodpile somewhere." Later, Gilmore demanded an apology. He never got one.

But this and other such similar comments by Billy about race should be weighed against his local record of supporting integration and busing his own kids to public schools. And there was an incident which occurred shortly after Christmas in 1966 which further supports the insight that there is more to Billy than meets the press.

Driving to work in his green Ford pickup, he heard on his CB radio that there was an accident outside of Plains. He was one of the first to reach the scene. Two cars had collided, and the worst injured of the victims was a little black baby who was bleeding badly. It was bitterly cold, so Billy took off his new suede jacket, a Christmas gift from Sybil, and carefully wrapped the baby in it. He held the baby against his warm chest until an ambulance arrived. Then he gently handed his suede-wrapped bundle to the attendant who raced the family to the hospital. Billy went home coatless.

He didn't tell Sybil what he had done because the jacket had cost her so much, but about a week after the accident the parents of the child appeared at the door to thank him and return his jacket. The baby was out of danger. They were very grateful to Billy for helping save her life. They had washed the suede jacket trying to get the blood out. It was ruined, of course, but Billy didn't mind. Neither did Sybil.

Like the girl with the curl in the middle of her forehead, when Billy is good, he is very, very good, and when he is bad he is awful. His short fuse caused him to blow again later in Jimmy's second gubernatorial campaign. He had been chafing under business pressures, and the more his brother advanced politically, the more the bureaucrats wanted to enforce what seemed to Billy to be stupid requirements. He had just lost an appeal on a federal requirement that he build an extra wall to reduce the sound level of the machinery outside the warehouse. Billy's comment: "Trains going through Plains, whistle blowing, have been waking people up for thirty years and the damn government wants to get rid of a little rumble that wouldn't wake a baby sleeping next to the warehouse." On top of this, there had been a lot of newsprint gossip about the candidate's wild brother. So Billy was in a gray mood when he attended an annual political gala thrown for the party faithfuls in Atlanta.

Hal Gulliver, then a columnist for the Atlanta *Constitution* (and now editor), was standing near Billy in the banquet hall and mentioned what another journalist had said about him. Billy thought Hal had personally made the comment and he exploded. Reeling around, he swung, hitting Hal solidly in the chest, sending him staggering. When Hal recovered he was more puzzled than angry, "Billy," he said, "I know you didn't really mean that." He knew Billy and he knew that he is impetuous but not vicious. But there was no justification for such a careless display of anger.

Reflecting on his conduct, Sybil once said to me, "I get so mad at Billy sometimes I almost want to strangle him. But I don't want anyone else to be angry at him or hurt him. If he gets hurt I can do it. I love him and I won't hurt him too much. I love Billy always, but I don't always like him."

I feel that way, too, but when I get upset with Billy, all I have to do is reflect on the many times he has been a good and trustworthy friend to me and others. In mid-1967, I was going through a very trying situation and I ran home to Plains. When Billy heard that I had shown up at Mother's in a distraught state, he came over immediately. I felt too threatened, too vulnerable to tell him what my crisis was. He thought I might need money, or at least that enough cash might allow me to do what I might need to do. He went to the bank and determined exactly how much he had and could raise in twenty-four hours. He told me the sum and said, "Ruth, if you need it, it's yours, all of it. I don't ever want you to be caught in a bind if I can help it." I didn't accept the money, but I did accept the love behind the offer.

When he is good, he is very, very good.

10

The Occupying
of Plains

In 1970, at the outset of his second attempt to become governor of Georgia, Jimmy told his volunteers, "Show me a good loser and I'll show you a loser. I don't intend to lose again!" Rising before dawn, he had his plans for the day down on paper by breakfast time. He worked until his final contact or speech of the day, which numbered sometimes as many as three, had been made. Late each night he headed home, dictating into a tape recorder politically useful information which Rosalynn would transcribe and file the next day. She made notes on information he might need immediately. She was no longer the shy, somewhat insecure nineteen-year-old girl he had married; she was a formidable campaign partner who was beginning to impress voters wherever she went in the state. And before election day, Jimmy, with her considerable aid, spoke in every city, town, and hamlet of Georgia. He alone gave more than 1,800 speeches. He and Rosalynn shook hands with some 600,000 people. And when the election votes were all in Jimmy had won it, big.

While Jimmy was in Atlanta, establishing zero base budgeting and shoring up the state economy, Billy was back home making some economic advances of his own. The warehouse was pulling in a gross of over $2.5 million a year and the Amoco station was doing a healthy $100,000 in trade annually—even though Billy was giving away more beer than he sold. As each succeeded on his own terms, the once-distant Carter brothers developed a greater mutual respect which would hold them in good stead when hard-ball national politics would threaten to undo their friendship.

Billy dug into a schedule he could live with. He was usually in bed by 10:00 P.M. and slept until 2:00 A.M. He then turned on a bed lamp which wouldn't disturb Sybil and started reading one of the four or five books he had going at the same time. His taste in literature ranges from notable works, like Tolstoy's *War and Peace,* to mystery stories by hack authors. At five-thirty he was ready to rise, dress, and begin his working day. He arrived at the warehouse at 6:00 A.M.

With the same dedicated workaholism that Jimmy exhibits, Billy plowed through each day, devoting all his energy to the business. But at 6:00 P.M. he usually left the peanut enterprise in the warehouse. The next two hours were his in the back room of the Amoco station with the boys. Then it was home to Sybil and his five handsome children, from Kim, the oldest, to the baby, Mandy.

There was a minor influx of tourists when Jimmy became governor. But Plains was essentially unchanged. About the only visible evidence that things were different was a large red, white, and blue sign over the block of storefronts on Main Street which read, "Plains, Ga.—Home of Governor Jimmy Carter." Beyond that it remained the same quiet, quaint southern village it had been since 1937, when Billy first arrived there. All that was destined to change.

When Jimmy told his brother that he was going to run for

President, Billy said, "I'll be damned." But he said nothing to discourage him. He let his feelings surface at the dinner table that night in June 1974. "Jimmy's sure bit off a hunk this time," he said to Sybil. Then, without looking up from the empty plate he had been staring at in silence for a few moments, Billy added, "But he might just do it."

The stakes were much higher, but the odds were the same as when Jimmy decided to run for governor. He wasn't even taken seriously by any but a very few friends who knew his drive and ability. And the idea stunned some of them. When Jimmy told Mother that he was going to run for President, she responded, "President of what?" He started the race far back in the field and no knowledgeable politician gave him an outside chance. They didn't reckon on his Olympian will to win or his skillful strategy. "Honey," Jimmy said to me in those early tough days, "I can will myself to sleep until 10:30 A.M. when I've been up til 1:00 A.M. and get my ass beat, or I can will myself to get up at 6:00 A.M. and become President." He got up at 6:00 A.M.

The first and perhaps most decisive part of his game plan was to run in every one of thirty state presidential primaries. Jackson, Bentsen, Bayh, Udall, Harris, Wallace, and, toward the end, Brown, all selected primaries where they thought they would make a good showing. Jimmy began with the first primary in Iowa—where he won—and he was in every primary after that.

When Jimmy started to win, suddenly the press began to search maps of Georgia for the location of Plains. They found it. And just as suddenly Billy was treated like a celebrity. It is impossible to describe the threatening feeling when this happens. Men and women armed with tape recorders, microphones, pencils, and pads descend on you. One day your conversation is not very important to anyone, not even your own family. The next day you find people recording your most casual comments, hoping to make headlines or at least copy for the national wire services.

Billy had his way of dealing with this plague. He told the reporters what he thought they wanted to hear. He created an image that would keep his heart anonymous as his name and cover antics went public. This is not to imply that Billy is actually a teetotaler or that he never really uttered anything bluer than "gosh" before the press showed up at his gas station. Rather he chose to exaggerate his vices and vitriol. The result was a public image which Billy soon found he was going to have to live with for a while. But many members of the press saw through his bluff and came to love him as much for the good-hearted person he is as for the good ole boy they helped to exaggerate, if not create.

Billy looked on with disbelief and foreboding as the philistine hordes set up their camp. On Highway 85 leading into Plains from Americus, just before you come to the Carter warehouses, in an empty lot on the left side of the road, three trailers laden with electronic communication equipment were rolled in. There was one from each of the major networks—ABC, CBS, and NBC. As Jimmy began to win more decisive primaries, more trailers from other television and radio networks, domestic and foreign, appeared. The empty lot was rechristened Television City. The news services moved into what had been Daddy's office in town. Banks of pay phones were installed for the reporters to file their daily stories. The occupation of Plains by the foreign invaders was complete.

So Billy decided to counterattack. He tried to defeat the enemy by feeding him great piles of baloney. He didn't realize until it was too late that these troops had lived on that diet so long they thrived on it.

They drank his beer, laughed at his jesting, and bought his redneck line. He was an appreciated comic relief in a political drama which can grow terribly boring and predictable. Early into a campaign, the working press assigned to cover daily developments can usually quote by memory what the major candidates are saying. I've stood in the back of an auditorium near the press and watched them mouth the speech Jimmy was giving for the fourth time that day. It is understandable why it was refreshing to cover Billy. He rarely took himself very seriously and often fed the press fabricated fun.

I remember one occasion when he ridiculed me on national television. I picked up an Atlanta *Constitution* in an airport recently, and there on the front page was my picture and a report of a TV interview with Billy who said he had had a hangover and came to me for prayer to get rid of it. "The prayer didn't work," he commented, "but three cans of beer did." I broke into laughter. The story was pure fiction. But I can imagine the consternation this impious remark created in many devout people who believe, as I do, in the power of prayer.

When Billy complained, "There's been so many damn lies come out of Plains lately it's changed the weather," he can take some of the blame for the clouds himself. But his fabrications were submitted in the spirit of fun. This is why he could never understand some of the deliberately malicious, harmful things a few reporters made up about him. The Atlanta *Constitution* ran a story which claimed that Billy had sold beer on Sunday at his Amoco station. If true, he would have been guilty of breaking a Georgia state law. But the true story exposed a journalistic license, not a crime committed by Billy.

A reporter looking for a good story—and evidently looking to make one up if he couldn't find a real one—came to Plains to interview Billy. It was early Sunday morning so Billy invited him to come into the back room of his now-famous gas station for the interview. The station was locked. So he opened it up, let his guest from the press in, locked the door behind him, and then settled down for the interview. As an act of second-natured hospitality he said, "How'd you like a beer?" The reporter eagerly accepted. He then proceeded to return the favor by handing Billy a cup of journalistic hemlock. He went home and made up the story that Billy had *sold* him a beer on Sunday.

Billy is a businessman, an excellent one, and those who knew him had nothing but contempt for that story. They knew that Billy would no more sell beer to a reporter in that setting than he would sell peanuts to Sybil. But in a matter of hours, one irresponsible reporter had succeeded in making Jimmy Carter's brother look like a two-bit scofflaw.

Billy's way of dealing with reporters is to launch into wild broadsides so preposterous that they have all the sting of a feather pillow. "About ninety-five percent of them would be on welfare if they weren't reporters," he once said. "And I still say that ninety-five percent of the writing reporters take the news off the AP and UPI. And about ninety-five percent of the television reporters get the information from producers. They don't know what in hell goes on. And, in fact, I've come to the conclusion the only reason anybody's a television reporter is because they can't read and write at all."

Take that! Pan the TV camera in on a cluster of excoriated, chastised, defamed, *laughing* reporters.

Billy writes off all TV anchormen as functional illiterates, except Walter Cronkite, whom he likes, and Mother adores. Like an Irish barroom brawler, he started with a legitimate beef, but when his verbal slugfest with the press warmed up, it got to be so much fun that he just kept swinging—long after he had any real cause to fight. Billy is enjoying the donnybrook. He delights in turning back serious questions submitted by the press with his wit.

A woman from Plains had been having a running feud with Billy, and in one of his frequent moments of delightful or disturbing candor, depending on whether you are hearing or receiving the verbal bruising, he said that if this particular woman died he wouldn't attend her funeral. Larry Knutson, an Associated Press reporter, heard that he had made the angry statement and decided to check out its accuracy.

"Billy," he asked, "is it true that you said you would never go to this woman's funeral if she died?"

"It's a damn lie," Billy protested. "I like funerals!"

The reporter made a few incoherent sounds. He knew he had just played straight man to Plains's W. C. Fields instead of achieving his investigative goal.

It was not long before Billy became a celebrity in his own right, and the subject of editorial comment. Perhaps the most perceptive of them was made by Arnold Rosenfield in his column in the Dayton *Daily News.* "Well, I *like* Billy Carter. I think he's smart and human, and that bluff exterior hides some very special hurts. I think it must be plenty tough to be the brother of somebody special, to be a living, walking, breathing, twenty-four-hour-a-day, full-time professional comparison.

"I think Billy Carter handles it in his own way—and pretty well."

Tom Tiede, of the Newspaper Enterprise Association, discussed the tendency of some members of the fourth estate to use Billy in an effort to spice up a story or humiliate Jimmy. But he missed the real Billy completely. "Everything Jimmy is, Billy isn't," he opined, "and the media knows from experience that this paradox has possibilities.

"Billy, beware," Tiede myopically warned. But all he does in such dark utterings is to show how profoundly he does not know Billy; he doesn't understand what makes him run. The truth is that Billy is a lot of things Jimmy is.

Tiede may have swallowed Billy's comment, "I'm not the Carter who never lies." A lot of people have, but those who have dealt with Billy where it counts in business and personal relationships know that he is as scrupulously honest as Jimmy. "I take a man at his word," Billy told another reporter. "In business, if anyone tells me he will do something, I expect him to do it, and he can expect me to do the same." This comment gives a more accurate glimpse of the man who lies about lying for the gullible who have acquired a taste for Southern-Fried Billy Carter.

It also became obvious to those who really know him that Billy soon began to feel uncomfortable with the "redneck" label. In an interview with Billy on the "Who's Who" program, Dan Rather got beneath the veneer with, "You said to me yesterday that you thought you might have created a Frankenstein monster. What did you mean?"

"I think I may have with my—I won't say act—but with my redneck pose," Billy responded. "I don't know what to do with it now." On another occasion, he said that the difference between a "redneck" and a "good ole boy" is that a redneck will drink a can of beer and then throw it by the side of the road; a good ole boy will be sure to throw it in the garbage after he drinks it.

That was Billy's way of taking his halo off. It would give him a headache to wear one. What he was really saying is, "A good ole boy cares." After a lifetime of observation, it is clear to me that Billy cares more than most people. People are important to him. You would never hear him say, "I don't throw my beer cans by the side of the road because I care about people and I want them to enjoy the countryside, not endure it." But that is what his down-home beer can, redneck statement was all about.

When it looked like Jimmy was gaining an insurmountable lead in the primary delegate count, a stop-Jimmy movement began to develop. A lot of established Democratic leaders were afraid of this political unknown. He owed no political debts which allows an officeholder greater freedom to move and less likelihood of yielding to corrupt influences. But it also leaves the establishment shaky about which way such a person may move. Jimmy was hurting. He was losing momentum.

Jimmy's children and, with special success, Rosalynn were campaigning vigorously for him. Billy also stepped up his appearances, and a poll by Jimmy's organization showed that he was definitely helping the cause. Nevertheless, campaign staff members often got upset with his drinking and his frank remarks to the press. How did Billy respond to this criticism? "I just tell them to go to hell."

Billy knew that, at times, Jimmy was concerned about him, but Jimmy never uttered a word of disapproval to him, nor in any way tried to change his life-style. One of the few times Jimmy got upset with Billy was just before the Ohio primary. Billy, with most of the family, had been deployed to Ohio to campaign in order to make a concerted last-ditch effort in this very crucial state. Shortly after Billy and his son, Buddy, arrived, they crossed paths on the campaign trail with the Udall forces. Harry, Congressman Udall's son, and Billy met. It was instant, warm friendship. The story that got back to Jimmy was that they joined forces and for the remainder of the time spent in Ohio, Billy and Harry campaigned together—one day for Jimmy and the next day for Mr. Udall.

It was a ball for Billy, but it angered Jimmy. You just don't win elections by campaigning for your opponent. But his laissez-faire attitude is so much a part of Billy that he couldn't adjust, not even for Jimmy. Sybil says Billy has always been this way, even in the early days of their marriage. Wherever Billy goes, people seem to let down their guard and begin to enjoy themselves. He has a way of making everyone feel comfortable and important. Billy sees it as a minor vice. "I've got a bad habit," he confesses. "I make my own party wherever I go."

Billy marched to another drummer while a slow-moving bandwagon was carrying Jimmy to New York and the nomination.

11

The Big Apple

With Jimmy's presidential nomination assured after the primaries, the stage was set for Billy's convention ball. There are few gatherings as stuffy as a national presidential convention. The windy, hot air predicted in the July weather report on the day of our arrival in New York was a prophesy of the social climate we sometimes had to live in for the next few days.

As I entered the Americana hotel, I was jostled through herds of conventioneers moving through the lobby. The noisy traffic of the city echoed against the chic but sterile hotel walls. Not a minute too soon, I found refuge in my room. But even there I heard the distant, muffled sound of horns blowing and the shrill notes of sirens punctuating the drone of endless streams of cars in the streets.

I had just received word that Billy had arrived in the city, and he had brought his Good Ole Boy Mafia with him as his protection against homesickness. I was anxious to see him since I knew it was his first trip to New York and he is still my *little* brother.

Nothing short of the prospect of Jimmy's nomination by the

111

Democratic National Convention could have lured Billy from
Plains to the boisterous Big Apple. As much as he hated the
"Miamiizing" of his hometown, he was still more at home there
than anywhere else. But Plains was going downhill fast. Mother
once observed to a reporter that in the "before-Jimmy days" a
dog could sleep in the middle of the street and never be awak-
ened all day. Now over two thousand tourists poured into
Plains each day. And it had become increasingly difficult for
Billy to maintain the low-keyed pace Plains once knew. His
efforts seemed futile—like trying to empty the ocean with a beer
can.

I dialed his room. Sybil answered. Her bright, familiar voice
embraced me, and I thought, "How I love that lady." She told
me that Billy had left immediately after arriving to case the
hotel and find all his new friends in the press corps. No one in
the Carter family is more liked by the working press than Billy.
I gathered up my purse and headed straight for the press room.
Sure enough, there he was. We hugged and then he asked,
"Have you had lunch yet?" I hadn't because I had been waiting
to see him. We went back to his room to get Sybil and then
down the elevator to the lobby where we inquired about a good
place to eat. "There's a great little restaurant right across from
the hotel," a friendly informant told us. We walked out of the
Americana hotel onto Seventh Avenue. A car whisked by Billy
at the corner as he stepped off the curb into the street, and he
stumbled backward to avoid being hit. Staring at the mass of
moving vehicles, Billy said, "My God, the traffic is almost as
bad as Plains."

The convention days for most of the Carters were filled with
parties from morning until night. Jimmy spent most of his time
in conference. There was still the final work of selecting the
vice-presidential nominee, and there was a constant stream of
staff members, governors, and congressmen in and out of

Jimmy's suite. Members of the family were asked to represent him at some of the social activities where he was supposed to make an appearance but couldn't due to the minute-by-minute strategy and vice-presidential considerations.

So each morning we were assigned our social commitments for the day. At first Billy was a little hesitant, but even he began to enjoy the new faces and the festive atmosphere of the convention. "I've never heard anything good about New York City in my life," he told one reporter when questioned about his reaction to the city, "but since I've been here I haven't seen one bad thing about it. It's been my biggest surprise." New York was winning Billy's heart and he was winning New York's. "My only complaint about your city is you can't get a can of beer for less than $1.15," he said. "That's enough to make anyone move out." The next morning ten cases of beer arrived at Billy's hotel room. With each successive day, the number of cases increased until his suite looked like a brewery warehouse. Billy got the message—"From New York with love."

On his second night in the city, Billy announced to the family that he was not going to any convention functions. "I'm going out to eat with a friend. He's a business associate and somebody's got to keep the peanut business together for Jimmy in case he loses." Billy invited one of his best friends, Tommy Butler, and his wife, Helen, to go with him and Sybil. They met his business associate at the entrance of an elegant French restaurant. Billy arrived in his yellow leisure suit and matching brown sport shirt. As they exchanged greetings and asked for their reservations, the maitre d' came up to Billy and said, "I'm sorry, sir, you must have a tie." Billy looked down at his leisure suit, thinking how ridiculous he would look had he worn a tie with that outfit. But he was in no mood to fight the dress code. "I'll be happy to wear one," he replied, "if you've got one. But I'm not about to go back to the hotel and get it."

"Yes, sir, I'm sure we can accommodate you." The maitre d' left the group and began his search. Minutes later he returned without the required tie. He looked as though he wished he had never broached the subject. It was plain to see he didn't want to turn Billy away, and yet rules are rules, even silly ones.

"What's that little thing hanging around your neck for?" Billy asked. The maitre d' looked down at his black string tie. Obviously it was the only way out of his dilemma. So he took off his little black string and dutifully tied it around Billy's neck. Now properly attired, he was ushered into the dining room with his friends. "What in the hell is this world coming to!" he mumbled.

The wine list was passed and everyone made his selection. Billy was a little unnerved when the wine was served. His was a different color from everyone else's. Turning to Tommy after his first sip, he whispered, "I thought I'd made a mistake when I saw my wine was different from the rest, but I *knew* I'd made a mistake when I tasted it. It tastes like half flat Bud and half you-know-what."

The waiter came over and gave everyone at the table a menu with each dish a gourmet special described in French. Billy took one look at it and growled, "The damn thing isn't written in English." As if this weren't enough for a regular customer at Fay's Cafe in Plains, there weren't any prices listed either. He could do without all this Gallic trick-or-treat. Glancing down through the list, Billy's finger hit a line of jumbled letters and he said, "I'll have this, please."

When his order was served, it didn't look too good. Billy stabbed a chunk of the gray brown something and put it in his mouth. It was awful. But he courageously continued to undo his humble, southern palate, and when he had finished the last bite, the food struck back at his contempt. Nauseous, he asked to be excused and nodded for Tommy to come with him. As he started down the steps to the rest room, he stopped by the waiter and asked, "Could you tell me what I just ate?"

"Yes, sir, you had goose liver."

No wonder I'm sick, Billy thought, and raced to the rest room. When Tommy caught up with him, he was retching over the commode saying between gasps, "Tommy, I ate it. I can't believe I ate the whole thing. I've eaten a plate of goose liver and I'd sooner eat dog shit." Tommy was hysterical.

There's no better game played in Plains by Billy and his buddies than to put one over on each other, or even better still, to see someone else do it. Tommy saw a good thing going and decided to push it a little more. "Oh, by the way, Billy," he said, "your friend wants to see you. He went to pay the bill and it was a little over $700 for the five of us, and he's left his billfold at home. That's what took me so long getting down here. He's embarrassed and wants you to come to the desk and pay the check."

Billy was now standing before the toilet staring at the wall and when Tommy's words registered, he spun around in his direction. He was a picture of put-upon humanity. "One thing's for sure," he said, "I'll stick to those damn convention parties from now on. At least you don't get poisoned." He splashed cold water on his face, took several deep breaths, and dejectedly reached for his billfold to count the cash. "What a hell of a night!" he groaned. Tommy couldn't keep a straight face any longer. The bill had already been paid and everyone was waiting patiently, he finally confessed.

As they returned to their table, Billy asked Tommy, "Where's that Mater-day?" Tommy pointed him out. Billy walked over and said, "Could I please have a menu to take with me?"

"*Ah, oui, monsieur,*" he said, looking very pleased that the night had been one Mr. Carter wanted to remember. "I'll get one for you right away to take back to Plains for a souvenir."

"Souvenir, hell!" Billy answered. "I want to take the damn thing home to study 'cause I'm going to learn the French words for goose liver before I come back so I won't ever make the mistake of ordering it again."

Bon appetit!

12

Mr. Carter

The three months between Jimmy's nomination and election were long, trying, and sometimes torturous. Life was rarely normal for any of the Carter family. I had scheduled speaking engagements related to my work in Inner Healing, and because of its personal, spiritual nature, I vowed I would never use any of these situations to campaign for Jimmy. I kept that vow, although it was very difficult because I was almost always asked questions about his candidacy. I also tried scrupulously to refrain from talking about my work when on the campaign trail.

Billy was never that cautious. His feisty independence was rarely tempered by the presidential campaign. When asked by reporters what he thought of Jimmy's controversial interview in *Playboy* magazine, he said, "I sent a boy to Americus with twenty dollars to buy some *Playboy* magazines. They were all sold out, so the kid bought twenty dollars worth of dirty magazines and I still don't know what Jimmy said. But I sure do have a lot of dirty magazines if you want to see what *they're* saying."

A minor crisis arose in Plains in the early weeks of the campaign. Down where the Seaboard Railroad tracks cut through town intersecting Bronwood Road, there is the old railroad station. It is a relic of the past, a mid-Victorian wood-frame structure which once served as the transportation hub of an earlier, peaceful Plains. As Jimmy's presidential campaign started into high gear, the old depot was selected to be his campaign headquarters. Some refurbishing, including a fresh coat of white paint with green trim on the exterior, transformed the drab, unused station into a handsome restoration out of village America, as well as the unique local headquarters for the "Jimmy Carter for President" campaign.

The day neared for the official opening of the headquarters, and Maxine Reese, amiable chairman—they don't use "chairperson" in Plains—of the committee which oversaw the depot redecoration project, gratefully accepted an offer from Reeves Construction Company of Plains to donate gravel to pave the dirt area around the station. When the huge gravel truck rolled up, Maxine stood behind it to guide the driver who was carefully backing to the spot where he was to dump the gravel. Inching backward, the truck suddenly began to list badly to the left, its rear tandem tires disappearing into the ground. It had rolled over the station septic tank and collapsed it. Billy came dog-trotting up to the scene. "What's goin' on?" he shouted. When he saw what it was, he had a good laugh, but Virgil Chambliss, lifelong Plainsite who came on the minor disaster about the same time, couldn't see the humor of the situation. "Why the hell didn't someone ask me?" he shouted. "I knew right where that septic tank was."

"Well, hell, Chambliss," Billy observed, "everybody in Plains knows where it is now."

The truck was towed out and the hole filled. It was the first, and the funniest, campaign crisis the town would weather. But it wasn't the last.

Billy was an effective, if not always eloquent, spokesman for his brother. At the height of the presidential campaign, he was invited to speak at a political rally in Danville, Virginia, and there he gave a speech that should be included in the *Guinness Book of World Records* as the shortest political speech in history. One politician after another preceded him, each trying to deliver lengthy barn-burners for their favorite candidate. It was all too much for Billy to bear. So when he was finally introduced, he smiled his happiest, eyes-all-aglow Pabst smile, and said, "Hiiiiiii!," waving slowly to the crowd with a beer can in his greeting hand. Then he sat down, amid roaring cheers!

Sybil was nearing full term in her last pregnancy as the presidential election approached, and there was more anticipation in their home over the new little Carter who was soon to arrive than the outcome at the polls. But when labor pains started, it wasn't just Billy and Sybil who slipped away quietly to the hospital. There was a whole retinue of Carters and friends: Chip and Caron Carter, Frances Irlbeck (Billy's secretary), Mother, Sybil's family, Billy's buddies, members of the press, and I think even a few tourists who joined the hospital-bound motorcade.

Sybil had chosen to have a midwife to assist the doctor. But some of her friends suspected she insisted on a midwife to help Billy, who informed the doctor he was going to be in on the delivery from beginning to end. When Billy and Sybil went into the hospital room, Marie, the midwife, was more than a little concerned about how Billy would respond to Sybil's pain. She was sure he would be traumatized by the actual delivery.

"Now, Billy," she instructed him, "put on this sterilized suit and mask. And as soon as you get them on, sit on the floor. No one's going to have time to stop and help if you pass out. And if you faint while you're sitting, it won't hurt as much."

Billy didn't pay any attention. He was too busy running back and forth to the family, friends, and neighbors in the waiting room, giving them his latest guesstimate on the arrival time.

"They're four minutes apart," Billy reported. "She's starting to sweat." The truth is, perspiration was pouring off his forehead and Sybil was a cool pro—and in almost no pain.

"Three minutes apart," Billy ran to tell the group. Then back again to Sybil's room.

"Billy," the midwife said, "I think you'd better suit up."

"Oh, God! It's coming," Sybil said.

"Move over to the delivery table," the midwife told Sybil, drawing the table up beside her bed. "Billy, damn it, put on that sterilized uniform," she shouted. She was beginning to lose her cool a bit. Dr. Gatewood, Sybil's doctor, hadn't arrived yet.

Billy grabbed his green hospital suit and struggled to get one leg in the pants.

"Don't move me," Sybil said. "I feel the baby coming." The phone started ringing. Sybil began to moan.

"My God, the baby is coming!" the midwife shouted.

All Billy could think of was getting that suit on. He started struggling with the coat and stuck his right arm through the sleeve. With only one pants leg on and one arm in the coat, he looked like a slapstick comic. He was just picking up the mask as the blessed event occurred.

Billy forgot all about the suit when he saw his new baby son.

"Oh, hell!" he shouted, "I can't believe it!" He reached down and grabbed Sybil around the neck. "We did it, Sybil, we had a boy!"

Sybil started laughing. Billy was laughing. And the midwife was crying.

"The doctor never got here," Sybil said, "but it really doesn't matter. We didn't deliver the baby; the baby delivered us!"

The phone which had begun ringing when the baby started coming was still ringing. Holding Sybil around the neck with one arm, Billy reached for it with the other—and shouted, "We don't have time to talk now because we've just had a baby." He slammed down the receiver.

The caller was Dr. Gatewood, the intended attending physician. He got all the information he needed. The baby, Earl Carter, was born.

The next great event in the Carter family occurred on November 2, 1976. Election night was kaleidoscopic. In room 1522, the Presidential Suite of Atlanta's posh new hotel, the Omni, Jimmy and the family were settled in for the agonizing wait.

Jimmy had conditioned himself to face emotional moments with incredible self-control. There was no hint of the feelings which surely flooded his insides. He looked like he was watching the weather report as he lay sprawled on a couch in front of three television sets, each with a different network reporting the early returns. Rosalynn's worry was as obvious as Jimmy's was concealed. She had worked so very hard campaigning for her husband. Her lovely face showed traces of strain and anxiety.

Their young daughter, Amy, and her girl friend, Laura, were nonstop from one room to another. How much history can two nine-year-old girls appreciate? The hotel had sent up a yellow sheet cake decorated with a sugar map of Georgia and a gaudy icing advertisement for the hotel which spelled out in large block letters OMNI. Amy decided the map was worth saving as a souvenir, but after she carefully lifted it off the cake and was heading for the bathroom to wash off the icing still clinging to the bottom, she tripped on the coffee table and fell. The map was reduced to a jigsaw puzzle on the top of the table, and Amy dissolved into tears. Rosalynn took her daughter into her arms and consoled her.

For most of the campaign kingpins it was a night of helpless suspense. They couldn't file a report, call an advance man, or wring another vote out of a state. For Hamilton Jordan and company, it was all over. The activity was swirling around Pat Caddell, Jimmy's pollster. Pat and his aides were down on their knees in a circle around the coffee table, interpreting figures from their field reports, or scurrying to and from two bedrooms where telephones had been set up for their final election-night prognosis.

Everything looked promising until Texas went into the Republican column. That set off an epidemic of anxiety. Up until that point, a festive atmosphere had been maintained, but it was gone now. The members of the family were less casual and moved more frequently to the TV sets. I found myself leaning toward the screen.

Jordan came in shortly after midnight and said, "I can't stand the suspense. I'm going to call Hawaii." Members of the Carter election team thought that Hawaii was securely in their camp and would take them over the top. A call was put through to Democratic headquarters in Honolulu. The race was neck and neck.

The networks had been laboring heroically to give their viewing audiences background color during the long wait. Nothing could be more colorful than Billy; so, predictably, there he was on one of the screens being interviewed in living color from Plains, a microphone in his face and a glass in his hand.

"Billy," the reporter queried, "how do you feel tonight about the possibility of your brother becoming President?" Flashing his cherubic smile, Billy replied, "I feel good tonight. In fact, I feel good most of the time." He was obviously feeling no pain. I glanced over at Jimmy to see his reaction. He was smiling.

"And what do you think," the reporter continued, "about the news that the race could still go either way?"

"I don't believe a damn thing I hear on television!" Billy

replied. "About 90 percent of reporters would be on welfare if they weren't reporters. Ten percent are okay." He was wearing a wide-angle grin and looking every bit a little boy. "You're in the ten percent," he said to the now-smiling reporter.

Several members of the family were watching Jimmy's expression, hoping he wouldn't show signs of irritation at his younger brother's candid comments. He seemed delighted. It really was the first break in the tension in too many hours.

The reporter fielded his final question. "If your brother wins, how will this change you?"

"There's one change I'd make," Billy answered. "If Jimmy does become President tonight, I'm gonna make everybody call me *Mr.* Carter for the first twenty-four hours. Then everything can be the same; I'll be Billy again after that."

The interview ended and once again the interminable tension had everyone in the room by the throat. At last at 3:28 A.M., the networks announced that Mississippi had given Jimmy the presidency. He leaped to his feet clapping and shouting, "All right!" Then he turned toward Rosalynn but didn't seem to be seeing anyone. "All right!" he shouted again.

I could not help reflecting to myself that this was the southern boy from Plains, Jimmy who?, the nobody who dared to believe in himself and the American people enough to rise from obscurity to the White House had done it. For twenty-two months of eighteen-hour days, he had walked, talked, ridden, and flown back and forth across this country to win the right to lead the nation he loves.

Hamilton Jordan let out a rebel war whoop that drowned out everything else for a moment. Then the entire room was flooded with sounds and motion: laughter, tears, everyone embracing everyone else, kisses, shouted congratulations and muted thank yous exchanged between Jimmy and those who had given the most to realize this victory. I looked over at him as Jody Powell went up to congratulate him. Jimmy gripped Jody by his shoulders, looking at him intently. His blue-gray eyes were filled with fatherly affection. I had no idea, until that moment, how deep the bond was between these two. Then they gave each other a profoundly moving bear hug. "Thank you," Jimmy whispered.

As the commotion began to subside, word was passed on to prepare for the trip down to the World Congress Center for the victory address. At 4:00 A.M. Jimmy walked into this cavernous auditorium the size of nine football fields. Over thirty thousand exhausted celebrants who had refused to leave broke into cheers and applause as he buoyantly stepped onto the stage holding Rosalynn's hand. He made a brief address and then headed out the door and on to his campaign plane, *Peanut One,* for the flight to Albany and the motorcade to Plains. That is where it had all begun, and that is where his celebration must end.

In Plains several hundred friends, neighbors, and Carter fans, who wanted to be at "the place" during election night, had been milling through the streets and around the train station for hours. Over 150 exhausted strangers had made their way to Billy's home. They had found that in this little town there was not only no room at the inn, there was no inn, or restaurants and, after 10:00 P.M., no public accommodations at all. Billy and Sybil decided to open their house to as many of these stranded strangers as possible. In an hour, two hams and two turkeys had been devoured, and the house was wall-to-wall people.

The flight in *Peanut One* was lighthearted and festive for the family in the forward section. Humorous stories about the campaign were exchanged, and it was so good to see Jimmy free of pressure for the first time in two years. He hadn't been able to show his warm sense of humor during those days, but it was back now. In the press section, exhaustion had caught up with the newsmen and women. They sat in almost total silence during the forty-minute flight.

At 5:30 A.M. we landed in Albany. Even at this dark, cold, predawn hour there was a small crowd waiting by the terminal building. As Jimmy emerged from the plane, they broke into cheers. We transferred to the waiting vehicles and, approaching Plains, we saw cars parked along the side of the road well over a mile before the city limits. When we arrived, the motorcade drove in behind the train station and to the rear of the platform which had been erected for this moment.

Jimmy and Rosalynn climbed the steps and crossed the stage to the podium. Mother was waiting for them. She was wearing one of the specially made football jerseys emblazoned with the words, "Jimmy Won" and the number 76. The proudest mother in the land went into her son's arms.

Billy was standing down at the edge of the steps leading up to the platform. His eyes were red from too little sleep and too much celebration. He just stood there looking up at his brother with a big, proud-as-punch grin on his face.

Jimmy stepped up behind the podium. His face was haggard, but his smile was radiant. The over five hundred people before him forgot the discomfort of the chilled morning air. The light of the sun was still beneath the horizon, but it revealed a bright, clear blue sky and the faces of many old friends in the crowd. Jimmy turned to his left where Billy was standing.

"*Mr.* Carter!" the President-elect said. "I want to thank you for waiting up all night to greet me." A thunderous cheer went up for Billy.

Jimmy then began to address family and friends. The television cameras allowed a nation to look in on this poignant moment. "I told you that I didn't intend to lose," he said in a voice that reflected both exhaustion and exultation. The crowd roared back its approval. The familiar scene of the stores and buildings freshly painted and decked out with red, white, and blue bunting, and the overwhelming love he felt from the people before him destroyed Jimmy's strong resolve to control his public display of emotion. He had not allowed himself the luxury of tears on camera in his whole long political career, but in this place, before these people, and at this great moment of joy, he was powerless to cover a well-spring of gratitude.

"I came through twenty-two months and I didn't choke up until . . ." Quick tears came to his eyes. He bit hard on his lip. He turned to his right where Rosalynn was already freely crying. He moved toward her, threw his arms around his beloved wife, and gave way to his own tears of love and thanks while the people applauded and shouted, and scores of friends around him laughed and wept.

At the very moment the sun broke over the horizon and sent a golden haze across the landscape, Jimmy said, "The sun is rising on a beautiful new day and there is a beautiful new spirit in this country, a beautiful new commitment to the future. I feel good about it, and I love every one of you."

And none did he love so gratefully as the brother who had stayed in Plains.

13

A Blue-Ribbon Candidate

The week following the election I was in Washington for the presidential prayer breakfast. A friend rode with me to the airport for my flight back to Fayetteville, and as we pulled up to the airport terminal, the cab driver turned around and spoke to me. "Pardon me, ma'am," he said, "I didn't mean to be eavesdropping but I couldn't help overhearing some of your conversation. You were talking mighty friendly about the President. Have you by any chance met him?"

"Yes," I replied, "I'm his sister."

"You're President Carter's sister?"

"Yes."

"Then, lady, you've got to be Billy's sister, too."

"That's right."

He opened the door of the cab, got out, and started shouting to all the drivers sitting in the cabs lined up in front of the terminal. "Hey, guys," he called out, "Billy Carter's sister is in my cab. Can you believe it? Come on over and meet her."

As my luggage was being unloaded by a skycap, the driver asked me, "Does Billy still have his Amoco station?"

"Oh, yes," I answered.

"Well," he said, "tell him to hang in there. We're all with him. And if he ever decides to run for President, there's a lot of us who'd give him our vote."

The whole country knows that "Roll out the Barrel" is Billy's song, not "Hail to the Chief." But Billy did decide to run for mayor of Plains two weeks later. As it turned out, he could have used some of those cab drivers' votes.

The campaign headquarters for the Billy Carter for Mayor race was the Amoco station. Not a speck of dust nor a dirty rag was removed to impress the electorate. "No Progress" was his slogan, and his station still stands as an example of prosperity without progress in a town gone dolled-up commercial for the tourists. Billy couldn't stand the thought of his Plains becoming Tinsel Town, or as he said, "a Miami Beach," and he had decided the best place to put the brakes on was in the mayor's office. His interest wasn't politics, it was Plains.

Back during the campaign, confident that Jimmy was going to win, Billy went with a delegation of local citizens to Johnson City, Texas. He wanted to see what officials there had done to protect Lyndon Johnson's birthplace from the blight of overexposure and exploitation. At a Texas-style barbecue—platter-size steaks, chili beans, and plenty of cold drinks—Billy sat down with Lady Bird Johnson to hear what had been done and what she recommended. He returned encouraged. Maybe there was still enough time, and as mayor perhaps he could steer the town on a more cautious course. But, clearly, he was very worried. "If something's not done," he warned, "the damn town's gonna be a junkyard. . . ."

Many outsiders couldn't understand what there was in Plains to save. Tourists were sometimes let down and a few even disgusted by what they found Plains to be—a few bleak wood-frame buildings lining a main street, and a water tower painted a gaudy red, white, and blue above an already huckster-blighted little town. What these people didn't see, as one writer explained, "is something so basic, so common, so typical, and so utterly undramatic that many visitors depart without ever realizing that what they are leaving behind on Georgia Highway 280 is an almost perfect, pristine example of village life in the American South." That is what Billy didn't want destroyed. That pristine village was his home.

The real Plains is not something a tourist could ever see. It is two hundred years of small-town life and death and all the colors of living between those two points. Hugh Carter, my first cousin, said to one reporter, "I believe a fellow could stay here a year or more and ask all the right questions and never get any right answers." It isn't because the citizens choose to be mysterious. Rather the people of Plains know that some things are nobody else's concern. Not really.

During the time of the mayoral race, over two thousand tourists were pouring into the town each day, and Billy was about the only businessman who wasn't selling peanuts or some kind of Carter memorabilia to visitors. There was already pressure from "outside money" to change the restrictive zoning laws, and that was just what Billy feared most. Buildings would start to rise everywhere. Motels, fast-food chains, boutiques, and tacky souvenir stands would make a rural tourist trap of our town. It was just this kind of disruption that Billy promised to curb. So with his "No Progress" slogan, his idea was not to turn the clock back, but to stand still long enough to control the growth and minimize the inevitable damage.

With tongue-in-cheek humor, Billy called an impromptu conference on the eve of the election. The reporters weren't exactly expecting a presidential press conference and they weren't disappointed. In mock anger Billy yelled at them, "You're all a bunch of illiterate turkeys. Nixon was right." They loved it. Most of them had never met a low-brow Will Rogers like him before. One reporter put it this way: "Billy is the only man I've ever met that when he tells you to go to hell, you feel such good stuff coming from his insides that you look forward to the trip."

As far as Billy was concerned, the press was the enemy, and the press conference was a running gun battle between the good guy, Billy, and the bad guys, the reporters.

"Do you have aspirations for higher office?" asked one bad guy. "Yes," answered the good guy. "I'm going to build an office upstairs so I can live a little higher." "Do you plan to maintain the culture of your city?" another bad guy inquired. "I'm not sure Plains has any culture," the good guy insisted. "Will you seek federal funds?" asked another philistine. "You always seek federal funds," was the sage's answer. "What will be your top priorities?" an illiterate turkey pressed. "To let the state government and the federal government do what they want to," said the literate pigeon, "and keep Plains out of it." "What happens if you lose?" asked a pessimistic pressman. "If I lose, I celebrate," answered the optimistic candidate. "And if you win?" a dreamer finally asked. "I celebrate. I promise you one thing I won't do. I won't get out and walk in the woods if I lose." That last response was a brotherly barb aimed at me. Billy was referring to the occasion when Jimmy and I took a walk in the woods after he was defeated in his first attempt to be governor of Georgia and the spiritual experience we had on that day.

Well, Billy went about the business of getting elected with an apparent political death wish. With his campaign manager, his buddy Leon Johnson, he stepped up his beer drinking. He promised that he would appoint only old cronies and political hacks to public office. And he guaranteed that he would have a press secretary who would make his remarks to the media people so off-color that they never could be printed. Mother predicted, "These churchgoers will never elect Billy mayor.

They're afraid he'll ruin their image." Ninety people were afraid of that anyway, whatever their religious persuasion. On election day, Billy succeeded in his drive to failure. He lost by nineteen votes—a landslide victory for his opponent, A. L. Blanton.

At Billy's defeat party on December 6, 1976, he lifted a can of Pabst and vowed, "I always keep my campaign promises." He had promised that he would celebrate if he lost, and he was certainly doing that. And win or lose, he had promised that the plastic Christmas tree A. L. Blanton had set up across the street from his Amoco station was coming down. A few days later, the tree mysteriously vanished without a trace.

The Georgia Bureau of Investigation questioned Billy. It was reported that the officers were smiling as they grilled the suspected criminal. The Americus *Times Recorder* displayed the headline PLAINS CHRISTMAS TREE STOLEN—BILLY HAD ALIBI. He did. All his friends testified that he was out of town the night of the crime.

The theft had been well planned. Someone placed a can of kerosene beside a car two blocks up the street from the plastic tree, and shortly after 7:00 that evening, another conspirator dropped a match into the can. The smoke drew everyone's attention away from the tree that was on Billy's hit list. As people watched the billowing smoke and the volunteer firemen rushed to extinguish the mysterious blaze, a car raced toward the tree. An unidentified tree rustler jumped out of the car with a lasso, and an expertly thrown arching loop of rope fell over the top of the eyesore. A jerk brought the rope tight, it was quickly tied to the back bumper, and what did wondering onlooking eyes behold but the getaway car fleeing from the scene with a Christmas tree bouncing behind it. That was the last anyone ever saw of the tree God didn't make and Billy couldn't take. Couldn't stand is more accurate. Everyone knows he could take it.

A few weeks after the Great Christmas Tree Theft, a reporter said to Billy, "I understand it cost you twenty-five dollars to have that tree stolen."

"It's a damn lie," Billy protested. But walking away, he said in a stage whisper, "It cost me a hundred dollars." Of course, he flatly denies he ever made this incriminating statement. The reporter denies it, too. It pays to have friends.

On December 20, Billy and his buddies set up a twenty-foot cedar Christmas tree to replace the plastic eyesore. The ornament at the top of the tree was—what else?—a beer can.

Billy's response to his defeat was predictable. With bittersweet humor, he said, "I lost because of the Baptist vote, the black vote, and the white vote." He then added, "It's really okay with me because to tell you the plain truth I think there are enough damn Carters holding public office."

No tears were shed by Billy's buddies. They knew that he was still the first citizen of Plains. The hottest-selling bumper sticker in the tourist-choked town confirmed their belief. It read, "PLAINS, GA.—HOME OF BILLY CARTER." In small letters beneath this proclamation were the two words: "and Jimmy."

Belly up to the bar, boys, Billy just got beat. The Amoco station back room had long been the unofficial clubhouse and pub for Billy and the boys. But now those days were over. One Sunday morning Billy climbed in his pickup and wheeled down to the station just to socialize with a few friends. The place was like the service area on a freeway. "It got so bad up at the station last Sunday that I couldn't even sneak a beer from the cooler," he complained. "Had to get a pint and ride around in my truck to find some peace and quiet."

His appearances at the station became less frequent, but wherever he went, he was greeted by a rush of excited sightseeing autograph seekers brandishing pens, pencils, and paper.

Billy couldn't understand what all the fuss was about. Why would anyone want his signature? "Unless it's on a five-cent check, it ain't worth a damn nickel."

A reporter asked Billy what he remembered most about the day he lost the election bid. "My losing the beer sales for the day," he replied.

That is not the truth. But it covers the sting of defeat with the salve of jest. Billy has too much goodwill to say to the press, "You'll never have Billy Carter to kick around anymore." What he seemed to be saying was, "I can't handle all the out-of-control, larger-than-life things that are happening to me. It's curl up and cry or stand up and laugh. So, let's laugh even if we have to laugh at me." And it is to the press's credit that, for the most part, reporters have sensed this and treated him with far more goodwill than antagonism.

In the Elkhart *Truth,* an Indiana paper, the editorial commenting on Billy's defeat affirmed, "Maybe the folks in Plains are so used to Billy that they don't appreciate him. Cheer up, Billy. It's a Plains loss. The rest of us love you."

14

The Inauguration

History was being made on the cold but bright, sunshiny day of January 20, 1977. Many months had been spent planning the details of Jimmy's inauguration and the other events of inaugural week in Washington. Staff members from the Carter headquarters had been sent to Washington long before the final balloting, and many more began to move from Atlanta to the capital after election day. So many details had to be taken care of: which singing groups would participate, how to house the 340 horses that were scheduled for the parade, making a guest list for the three hundred thousand invitations to be sent out. And then there were preparations to include two hundred musical events; Jimmy insisted on having music that would fit the tastes of everyone—from classical to country-and-western. There were also special events for the children, free tours, and parties and receptions galore for those in a festive mood.

Jimmy had asked for a simple, modest, inexpensive inauguration, yet he wanted all 215 million people in the United States to be involved. Having a "People's Inaugural" wasn't the easiest feat to accomplish. Andrew Jackson had tried it more than a century before and found that it presented a number of problems. Back then so many people came that they filled the hotels and were sleeping five to a bed. Invited to a reception at the White House, Jackson's "backwoods" buddies left it in a shambles.

Billy brought several of his buddies to Washington for the celebration on a chartered plane dubbed "The Georgia Redneck Special." Even an old friend of his from Marine boot training was part of the bash: Warrant Officer Dan Barth, who had remained in the Corps after the Korean War. All the members of the Carter family had been assigned officers to escort them while in Washington. But Billy objected when he was informed that his escort would be a colonel. He insisted on his good friend, Barth. So out went the usual protocol and Warrant Officer Barth it was.

Arrangements had been made to house the family at the Hilton hotel. But since there were eighty-seven family members, rooms on the ninth floor, the one set aside for the family, were at a premium. Billy asked for eight more rooms. The management balked. When told that only family would be staying on that floor, he said, and meant, "My buddies *are* my family." He got the rooms he needed for his friends. When he got his bill, they all kidded him about trying to buy a piece of the hotel. But again Billy laughed it off and hid his shock with a lighthearted, "I'll just send the bill to the White House."

When Billy first started making his plans to go to the inauguration, he called the airlines to charter a plane. There was some trouble at first because, as Billy says, "They told me it had to be a special event." "What's a special event?" he asked. And the reply was, "Like the Sugar Bowl." He knew it was useless to argue with anyone who thought a football game was more important than the presidential inauguration. So he called on his new friend Walter Mondale. When the Vice President-elect put in a call to Delta Airlines on Billy's behalf, the red tape vanished like a winning team's goalpost. Billy had no more trouble getting his plans together with the airline.

Over a hundred of Billy's fun-seeking friends made the trip, each of them paying $122 as his share of the charter which Billy had personally arranged with a little help from a friend. It was a day of unforgettable excitement for the pilgrims from Plains. For many of them it was their first airplane trip. Billy saw to it that the flight was well stocked with beer and champagne in case the plane's supply ran low. Most of the Amoco Mafia— Tommy, Bud, Randy Coleman, and Captain Brown Jordan— were there to enjoy it. While breakfast was being served on the flight, one of the reporters aboard interviewed Captain Jordan.

"And you are . . .?"

"Captain Brown Jordan. Yes, suh. Twenty-eight years with the Georgia State Patrol, now growing peanuts. Yes, suh. Ah just plant, spray, and pray. I got fifty-seven acres. Billy calls my spread Sin City."

"Er, right, Cap'n. Got a CB handle?"

"Yes, suh. Bra Jumper."

"How's that?"

"Bra. You know, like in hedgerow. Bra."

"Oh. *Briar* Jumper. What's that mean?"

"You obviously ain't a hunter, suh," said Captain Jordan, summoning up his best dumb-Yankee frown. "Means someone who goes quail hunting in rough country without thick britches."

That interview didn't make the society pages of the Washington *Post*. But the people on board the plane loved it.

By the time the "Redneck Special" landed, almost everyone on board was in a state of Southern Comfort. When Billy stepped off the plane, a Marine escort was waiting to take him by limousine to the hotel. But when he realized that he was the only one getting the VIP treatment, he refused to leave his friends. Instead, he took the bus with them to the hotel.

Before leaving the airport, Billy shook hands and posed for pictures in the terminal with some of the growing members of Billy Boosters who had recognized him. When asked by one of them what he felt about his brother becoming President, he suddenly grew serious. The puckish smile was gone. "I hate to see him get the damn job," Billy replied, "but I'm glad for him that he won. I just hate to lose him."

Billy knew it would never be the same again. His brother now belonged to the nation and history. The gulf of age, unintended conflict, and differing interests which had narrowed with time and business ties had widened again. And he couldn't hide his sense of loss.

The weather was cold that day in Washington. But Billy encouraged his thin-blooded Dixie friends with, "I hear it's gonna be 40 degrees here in Washington tomorrow for the inauguration. Jimmy must have been talkin' to the Lord again." He shrugged off the chill. Someone handed him an overcoat, but he refused it. "It's not cold up here," he said. "It's cold down in Plains, only 8 above zero." That was his way of saying he was going to miss his brother. Billy felt cold—all the way to his heart.

Curiously, I spent more time with Billy in long conversations during inaugural week than at any time since Jimmy started running for the presidency. All of the members of the Carter family, of course, attended the major events except Sybil, who caught a virus soon after arriving in Washington and was unable even to attend the inauguration ceremonies. That meant that Billy spent a lot of time near Sybil in their suite. Some reporters thought that he was partying constantly during that week—and there were parties in the suite. But it was then that Billy usually retreated into my room where we talked about life and everything else until sometimes as late as three o'clock in the morning. Billy and I have rarely been closer than during that time, and many of the things we talked about have come back to me in observing Billy and having some concern about his life since that eventful week.

On the same day that the "Redneck Special" landed, another member of the family, Jimmy, with Rosalynn and Amy, had arrived in Washington almost totally unnoticed. Traditionally, the President-elect comes to the capital with some considerable pomp and fanfare. Jimmy wanted none of it. His chartered jet was parked at some distance away from the main terminal at National Airport, and he came down the steps from the plane carrying a suitcase and a large, bulging green paper sack. He was greeted by a few reporters, cameramen, police, and the ubiquitous Secret Service, but quickly made his way to a chocolate brown Lincoln Continental that was waiting for them and helped Rosalynn pack the trunk and they drove off to Blair House.

On the evening of the inauguration, Jimmy changed from blue jeans and an open collar sport shirt to a tuxedo and black tie to attend a gala at the Kennedy Center. The evening proved to be one of the most colorful of a week of colorful celebrations. There was an air of subdued excitement as our family filed in to seats just to the right of the presidential box.

When Jimmy and Rosalynn came in and took their places, the people in the packed hall rose to their feet cheering and applauding. Jimmy's smile was 24-carat and Rosalynn looked as beautiful as I have ever seen her. I could sense how very proud she was of Jimmy, and she had great reason to be proud of herself. No one, not even Jimmy, had changed as much on the journey from Plains to Washington as the new First Lady. Few people knew how hard it had been for this basically shy country girl to assume the role of campaigner, public speaker, active politician, and adviser. But those who have watched her closely know that she has filled those roles with both necessary flair and substance. She had more than earned her right to stand next to Jimmy and accept the adulation they received that night.

When the cheers and applause finally began to fade, I gazed up at the glittering sunburst chandeliers of the Kennedy Center. They looked like giant golden brooches crafted by a jeweler, and I got that feeling again that it all just can't be true—my brother Jimmy was soon to become President of the United States.

That night was a parade of some of the most famous names of the entertainment world. Muhammad Ali, Paul Newman, Jean Stapleton, John Wayne, Loretta Lynn, and a host of other celebrities were there. Leonard Bernstein conducted the ninety-seven members of the National Symphony Orchestra in a new work he dedicated to Rosalynn. The seventy-six-year-old Aaron Copland bounced up and down on the podium like a country-and-western musician as he led the orchestra in a selection of his own works. James Dickey read a poem he had written for the occasion, "The Strength of Fields."

During the intermission I looked over toward Billy and exclaimed, "It's all pretty wonderful, but I've been so busy and I haven't had time to eat. I could certainly enjoy it more if I had just taken time out for dinner." The crowd began to move out into the halls to chat, to stretch, to smoke. Billy took me by the hand. "Come with me, Ruth." We threaded our way through the crowds down several flights of steps into a long hall and opened a door. Inside the room there was a big table filled with food. "Billy," I exclaimed, "how did you know about this?"

"Oh, well," he said, "I usually try to find out the important facts of life when I go any place." While we ate we had the

opportunity to visit with Senator Hubert Humphrey, Walter
Cronkite, and Roger Mudd. Yes, it was the CBS VIP lounge
—an oasis in the desert. Billy and I returned a little late for the
rising curtain, but having had something to eat, we were much
happier during the last half of the concert. We found out later
that Jimmy had spent the intermission conferring with his top
aides on the economic package he planned to present to Congress.

The day of the inauguration dawned crackling cold and clear.
I was weary from the night of festivities, but I had been invited
to offer a prayer at a special religious service to be held at the
Lincoln Memorial at 7:00 A.M. I bundled into about four layers
of clothing, exposing only boots and a red cape, but as I stepped
up to the podium I trembled—or was it the chill I felt from a
heart that was so overloaded with emotion?

I looked out into the sea of faces before me. Many of them
were familiar—old friends from Georgia and other places my
work had taken me. Seated just behind me was Martin Luther
King, Sr. This elder statesman of the black civil rights movement had shown unswerving loyalty to Jimmy. He believed in
him and had done everything in his power to convince the
blacks of America that the candidate from South Georgia was
their friend. It was fitting for the Reverend King to address the
people of America from the steps of the national shrine that had
been erected to honor the man who had ended slavery, and
where, from these same steps, his famous son had once spoken
of a dream he had of a land united in faith, love, and brother-
hood.

I left the Lincoln Memorial to join the rest of the immediate
family at the Baptist Church for prayer before we went to the
steps of the Capitol where the crowd was gathering for the
inauguration. It seemed to grow colder as the inaugural festivities got under way. But during the ceremony itself, the chill

seemed to lift for many of us. We felt only pride and hope as
we watched Jimmy take the Presidential Oath of Office with
Rosalynn standing by his side. I could see Mother biting her lip
as she often does when she is trying not to cry. I looked around
for Billy. He was there with his younger children, but Sybil had
stayed at the hotel, terribly ill with the twenty-four-hour virus
which affected most of us in the family during the week. I felt
numb. And then I heard these words in Jimmy's familiar voice:
"The American dream endures. We must once again have faith
in our country—and in one another. I believe America can be
better. We can be even stronger than before."

The weather turned even colder as we waited for the inaugural parade to begin. The sidewalks of Washington were crusted
with hard ice, and over two hundred soldiers had been working
steadily with sledgehammers, trying to crack the ice on Pennsylvania Avenue. The family sat together in the bleachers
across from Rosalynn and Jimmy, huddled close to each other
and covered with blankets, literally, from head to toe. Some
kind gentleman in the crowd had brought a large thermos of hot
wine which saved the day.

Just as the parade got underway, Gloria and I left the stands
to find a rest room. Ed Bradley of CBS was standing up on the
top row by a TV monitor. He motioned to us to come up
quickly. It wasn't very easy to ascend to the top, but we made
it.

"Look," he said, "the crowd is going wild—and I'll bet the
security is even wilder."

"Oh, no!" Gloria shouted. Jimmy, Rosalynn, and Amy were
not riding in a limousine as planned. They were *walking* down
the middle of Pennsylvania Avenue. I was only one among
many who began immediately to pray for their protection. Even
though the rest of the parade was magnificent, with 170 march-
ing units which included fifteen thousand persons, nothing

could top the emotion we felt seeing our First Family walking the one and a half miles from the Capitol to the White House.

The parade ended at 3:43 P.M., and the family gathered at a designated location to be ushered into the White House. We were all chilled to the bone as we stood waiting for the President and First Lady to make their entrance first. We wondered what the delay was until a security guard came up to inform us that the President wanted his family over with him. Jimmy had once again refused to follow protocol and said, "It was a family campaign and I want the family to all go in with me." We entered the White House together.

A small reception was planned for us on the second floor in the family living quarters, and then we all toured the White House. Sybil had joined us. She looked pale and held on to Billy's arm, but she was determined not to miss this part of the day. We soon noticed that Jimmy had disappeared, but we continued the tour until we came to the Oval Office. There, Michael, my son, walked over to the President's desk, sat down in the big chair behind it, and, holding up each hand with the victory sign, shouted, "We won, we won." Jimmy was standing at the far end of the room deep in conversation with Bert Lance and Cyrus Vance. He hadn't seen us come in and he turned around with a start. "Everyone had better leave now," he said. "I've got some work to do." His administration had already begun.

Michael, feeling he had done something wrong, wrote his uncle after he returned home to apologize for making noise and disturbing him. He addressed the letter to President Jimmy Carter—White House. Three days later there was a letter in the mail for Michael on official White House stationery from the President of the United States. He assured Michael that everything was all right and that he had not even remembered the intrusion. Then there was a P.S. at the end: "Michael, by the way, you do know you are the only one who sat in my chair before I did, don't you? Love, Uncle Jimmy."

After our brief tour we joined the other guests. The White House was beautiful. All of the rooms for the reception had been decorated by friends from Georgia, including members of Sybil's garden club in Plains. They had come early, bringing Georgia flowers they had been growing for the occasion. Tulips, camellias, snapdragons, poppies, roses, and greens filled the vases.

Seven inaugural parties were planned for that evening. Jimmy attended all the balls, but Billy and I went to only three. When we arrived at the ball our Georgia friends were attending, we never left. We got there just in time for Jimmy and Rosalynn's arrival. Jimmy walked through the crowd, seeing familiar faces, and greeting those friends who were so close to his heart. Tears were in his eyes as he walked up to the microphone and asked, "Are you having a good time?" There was a surging from the crowd and the cheers rang out, "Yes!"

"Do you believe in America?" he asked. We answered, "Yes!" again with even greater enthusiasm.

"Are you going to help me?" That time the windows seemed to rattle with our response.

Then Jimmy quietly took Rosalynn's hand and said, "Have a good time. I'm going to dance with my wife."

We all obeyed the presidential order to have a good time. Tonight we had a hero and there was a cause to celebrate. And celebrate we did.

I remember any number of odd and colorful things during that inauguration week. There was the man dressed as Abe Lincoln who appeared on roller skates and fell down in front of the reviewing stand during the parade. The expensive Sans Souci restaurant near the White House added a peanut butter sandwich for $6.50 to its menu. Someone told me there were new and wondrous songs on jukeboxes, presumably in semi-honor of the Georgians in town, like "Drop Kick Me, Jesus, Through the Goalposts of Life." One song, the "Redneck National Anthem," was probably played more than once with Billy in mind. But I remember, in particular, James Dickey's poem, "The Strength of Fields." The last line of the poem, referring to the new President, touched me. "My life belongs to the world. I will do what I can." I know how accurately that line reflected what was in Jimmy's heart.

15

Family Man

Billy, Sybil, and their children, and Gloria with her husband, Walter, returned to their business and friends in Plains after the inaugural celebration was over. I went back to Fayetteville to my family and my work. Mother returned home with her memories. Her world was Jimmy.

She had hardly settled into her rocking chair at the Pond House when she received a call from Jimmy. It was 8:00 A.M. "Mother," new President Carter said, "I'm coming home this weekend. Can you meet me Saturday morning in Macon and ride with me in the motorcade?" It was his first trip home since taking office. Macon is the location of an air force base and had the nearest landing facilities which could accommodate *Air Force One,* the President's plane. "Yes, Jimmy," Mother answered with little enthusiasm. "I think I can meet you." He told her he was anxious to see her again and ended the call.

Mother was feeling a little under the weather, so around nine o'clock she called Billy about Jimmy's arrival the next day. When she complained that she just didn't feel up to traveling all the way to Macon, Billy said, "Well, then don't go, Mother.

You can see Jimmy when he gets here."

That was all the support she needed. She asked a state trooper to get a note to the Secret Service which was to be delivered to President Carter. The note told him she wasn't feeling well and would be waiting to see him at the Pond House.

At noon Mother's phone rang.

"Hello."

"Mother, this is Jimmy again."

"Well, Jimmy, what is it?"

"Mother, how would you like to go to India?"

"Son, you know that I said last year there are only two things I greatly desire in life. One was to see you elected President. The other was to return on a visit to India."

Her two years of Peace Corps service in India had permanently endeared the people of that great subcontinent to her. She had often expressed her wish to see the people of the village of Godres where she had nursed and helped build the community's first adequate medical facility.

"Can you be ready to leave for India by three this afternoon?" Jimmy said.

Silence.

When at last Mother spoke, her voice had risen, and there was an edge of excitement as she said, "Yes, I think I can. But who will buy the ticket, you or me?"

Jimmy quietly laughed. "It's not like that, Mother," he said. "The President of India has just died, as you probably heard on the news, and you are going to his funeral as my personal representative. The government will provide the plane." He told Mother that a government jet would be waiting at the Albany airport at 3:00 P.M. to fly her to Washington where she would depart for India.

The elixir of a dream fulfilled cured Mother's illness. She was feeling very good quite suddenly. She picked up the phone and

dialed Billy. "I'm going to India this afternoon," she announced.

"You sober, Mother?"

"Jimmy just asked me to go for him," Mother replied.

Billy knows better than ever to question this globe-trotting
grandmother about her travel plans. "Have a good trip," was
all he could say.

A few moments later Mother received another call from the
White House protocol officer asking her if she owned a floor-
length black dress, the necessary attire for the funeral. Of
course, she didn't.

When she arrived at Washington National Airport at five
o'clock that afternoon, a fashion coordinator and a seamstress
from Garfinkel's Department Store had three dresses at the
terminal. The first one Mother tried on looked as if it had been
tailored for her. The seamstress swiftly hemmed it to the right
length and within the hour America's First Mother was flying
to her beloved India. She felt just fine.

It became clear to Billy and Sybil shortly after the inauguration that they wouldn't be able to remain in their rambling old
weathered-white wood-frame house in Plains. The heap of livin'
that makes a house a home had been put into the place years
ago. As their family grew and as their budget would allow, they
had added on a wing in the back with a spacious family room
and a large ranch-style kitchen with an early American table to
accommodate the whole household and frequent guests. This
addition replaced the cramped quarters that had little space for
more than the sink, stove, and refrigerator, and Sybil made sure
the new kitchen had lots of cupboards. These changes also
allowed them to tear out a couple of interior walls to add a
bedroom for their expanding brood.

Comfort and livability aren't easy in a three-bedroom house

with six children, but Sybil was somehow able to create these qualities. She and Billy were happy living there until they were pressured to leave by the tourist invasion.

It wasn't unusual for Sybil to walk into the front of the house and see a curious out-of-towner peering through the window, or to have a cluster of strangers standing at the edge of their front yard waiting with cameras in hand to take a picture of any real live Carter who might emerge from the house. Once-simple experiences like a trip to the grocery store two blocks away became an unnerving ordeal. Sybil was besieged by badgering autograph seekers and curious questioners, and Billy couldn't put a foot out of the house in daylight without being almost stampeded by people.

In February 1977, they decided to look for a house in Buena Vista, a very small town nineteen miles from Plains. Their children were attending school there, and it would not be difficult for Billy to commute to the warehouse. They thought they would rent until they could build somewhere in the area.

Shortly after Sybil started to search for a place, she heard about a young couple who had just built a beautiful, spacious contemporary home set in the middle of a sixty-acre plot of land near Buena Vista, but, who, for personal reasons, now wanted to sell it. One day Billy and Sybil drove down to see it, but not without difficulty. Even with the directions it was a very hard place to find. However, after turning off one road and driving down another for about a quarter of a mile through a thick stand of southern pine, they beheld the house standing in a clearing at the top of a high, gently rising knoll.

Inside the house they were greeted by a spacious, high-ceiling entrance way which led into a formal dining room on the left, and on the right a beautiful walnut-panelled library-den with a stove fireplace attached to a master bedroom. They walked past a large country kitchen, and at the end of the hall there was a massive living room with brown-stained exposed beams and large picture windows looking out on a terrace. Up the broad, thickly carpeted staircase were three more bedrooms.

This might be the place to buy, they thought, but they decided to sleep on it. The next day Sybil returned to the house alone. Another tour almost settled it in her mind. But she wanted Billy to take another look at it and make the final decision. So the following day he piled into his pickup and headed for Buena Vista. About an hour later Sybil's phone rang. "Sybil," the harried voice on the other end said, "I can't find the damn house." She told him she would drive down and lead him to it. Billy wanted a house that would provide his family with privacy. This house gave him, at the moment, more of that than he knew what to do with.

After Sybil met Billy and they went through the house on the hill one more time, they agreed that this would be their new home. They bought the house on Wednesday and moved in on the following Monday.

Not long after, I went to Plains from my home in Fayetteville to see Sybil. A local police officer had to show me the way to their new home. It was beautiful on the outside, and once inside I was alternately impressed by the house's loveliness and the nonstop family activity swirling around me. Billy was in Washington, D.C., talking with Jimmy, and was due to arrive back late the next day. Sybil was happily laying out the main ingredients in preparation for a luncheon the next day for thirty people. Tom T. Hall and his band were coming to entertain family and friends.

Billy showed up unexpectedly the following morning. Sybil and I were in the kitchen working when he arrived. He came in with a 200-watt smile, kissed Sybil, and then gave me a warm hug. His first question was, "Where's Earl?" He wanted to hold his eight-month-old son.

Billy's children have always been a source of pleasure and pride to him. He is quick to give Sybil the credit for their high quality—and she deserves high marks for motherhood—but Billy has been a devoted, loving daddy. And although he was shamefully spoiled by our family, he has been a firm disciplinarian with his own children. There has never been any doubt in their minds that he adores them, but he can still be tough. The phrase they hear from his lips more often than any, his catch-all cliché, is an optimistic, "Well, good!" "I'm upset with you, Daddy." "Well, good!" "I wish I didn't have to do my homework." "Well, good!" They had better do their homework. The "Well, good!" is just diplomacy before discipline if a heavy hand is needed. They know better than to think "Well, good!" means, "Well, forget it."

Earl is the exception, so far at least. That baby is pampered and waited on by Billy and every other member of the household. Sybil told him that Earl was in his bedroom asleep. Billy went in, lifted the baby out of his crib, and carried him back into the kitchen.

Sitting with his son in his lap, he began to review the highlights of his trip away from home. It had been his first personal visit to the White House and it had a disastrous beginning. He took a cab from Washington National Airport, and when he arrived at 1600 Pennsylvania Avenue, he made it easily through the East Gate after the Secret Service gave him a quick once over. But that was where the well-oiled White House machinery stopped. Once inside the building, he told an aide to Tim Kraft, Jimmy's appointments secretary, that President Carter was expecting him. The clerk said he was sorry but the President was busy all day and it wouldn't be possible for Billy to see him. Obviously that civil servant was out of touch. But Billy is a proud man. He wasn't about to plead to see his own brother. So without any outward reaction to this glaring example of

An old photo of downtown Plains, Georgia, in the early
1920s, when Mother and Daddy were first married.

My older brother and sister, Jimmy and Gloria,
about the time I was born.

This picture of me must have been
taken when I was about ten.

My brother Billy on our farm
outside of Plains.

Our house at the farm.

Jimmy and our little brother, Billy.

Billy and his sweetheart, Sybil,
early in their high school years.

Billy and Sybil in their formal wedding picture.

Billy in the Big Apple during the
Democratic Convention, 1976.

Billy campaigning for Mayor of Plains.

Billy, Mother, and Jimmy at a family reunion in Plains.

Billy and Sybil together at home.

Billy and me at the wedding of Jana Kae Carter,
Billy and Sybil's daughter.

impertinent bureaucracy, he walked out and checked into a motel.

When word filtered through to Jimmy of what had happened, his eyes turned to that cold steel gray which signals to anyone who knows him that his carefully disciplined emotions are feeling something close to fury. He got on the phone and traced his brother down. He told Billy how sorry he was for this needless slipup and would he please stay at the White House. When Billy said he would, a driver was sent to pick him up, and he started to check out only to find that Jimmy had already called and taken care of everything. Affairs of state were now so pressing that Billy and Jimmy could not spend too much time doing their necessary catching up. It was simply a matter of first things first. Short of a national crisis, Jimmy would never put his brother off if he came to see him.

That night Billy slept in the Lincoln Bedroom, he told us, and early the next morning he went down to the press room to share a cup of coffee with the reporters. One of them ribbed him saying, "Billy, don't you think you cost the government a lot of money staying at the White House?" Billy was all grin as he told us, "I said to him, 'It couldn't have cost much because I got up early and washed all my sheets and towels. I didn't even order up a cup of coffee. I came down here to get it free off you fellows. But I didn't do that just to economize; my real reason was I didn't want the ghost of President Lincoln to come out and haunt this southern boy for messing up his room.' " End of interview.

Billy's next stop was an appearance at a Kiwanis International Convention in North Carolina, and Sybil wanted to know why he was home early. "I thought you weren't going to get home until tonight," she said.

"Well, I couldn't sleep last night," Billy explained. "Those convention fellas kept knocking at my door asking to meet me and party. And I didn't want to party. I wanted to sleep. So about four this morning I checked out, went to the airport, and caught a plane for Atlanta."

"But how'd you get from Atlanta to here so fast?" Sybil asked.

"I drove seventy all the way, that's how."

"Billy Carter, you could have killed yourself. You make me so mad."

Billy lifted Earl anxiously. His lap was wet. "I think—ah—someone better change the baby," he said sheepishly.

Kim, their twenty-year-old daughter, was standing at the door leading into the hall. "I'll take him, Daddy," she said. Kim is much like her mother in temperament. She has a cover-girl beauty with long, casually coiffed blond hair and sparkling blue eyes. A melodic voice rounds out the picture, but she has a will of steel when she is challenged and feels she is right. She is no glamorous Dixie honeysuckle pushover. Just like Sybil, she has a mind and will as strong as any.

Only three months ago she had demonstrated this strength. She is a member of the Plains Baptist Church, and when the meeting was called by the deacons to decide whether to retain or fire their young pastor, Bruce Edwards, because he refused to support the church's segregation policy, Kim was determined to be there. She was the only member of Billy's family to attend the meeting. Sybil had a new baby and everyone knows what Billy thinks of the church.

Kim sat in stunned disbelief as angry bigots shouted down those who supported Reverend Edwards and integration. At last she stood at her seat in the back of the sanctuary and spoke with a voice choked with emotion.

"I have always loved my church," she said, "and I have tried to faithfully support it. But if you dismiss Reverend Edwards and refuse to allow blacks to enter this sanctuary, I will never come back to worship with this congregation. I'll not remove my membership because this is my church and it will always be. But when I marry I intend to marry in this church. My best friend is a black girl with a beautiful singing voice. I've always wanted her to sing at my wedding. And I want all of you to know that if you won't let her come into this church, I'll have her stand on the steps and sing. I've always thought the reason for coming to church was to worship God in the name of Jesus Christ. It's obvious that some of you have forgotten Him completely."

The once-shouting Christians who had lost their way sat in silence. They still voted to oust Reverend Edwards, but Kim's honest, forceful support of the truth made their action all the more ugly and inexcusable.

As Sybil continued her party preparations and Billy stood up to leave the kitchen, Buddy, his oldest son, came in followed by two of his high-school friends. Billy was going to pick up the Tom T. Hall band at a motel in Americus within the hour.

"Daddy," said Buddy, "may I stay over at Johnny's after the Junior-Senior Prom tonight?"

"Well, with all the guests staying here tonight we could use your room. So, it's okay with me."

"Alllllrrrriiiiiggghhttt!" a pleased Buddy exclaimed.

As I looked at this handsome, friendly sixteen-year-old with almost white-blond hair, I felt my age a bit. It seemed only a very few yesterdays that he had been born. William Alton Carter IV had been born in 1960, and as he disappeared out the door, Billy said proudly, "He's sure a chip off my old block."

"Your humility overwhelms me," I laughed. But it was true. Buddy had recently acted like a six-foot carbon copy of his daddy's reaction to his White House snub.

Back in the summer of 1976, Billy had purchased the available property around Jimmy's house when his presidency seemed a likelihood. He knew it would be necessary to protect the privacy of Jimmy's house. After the land was acquired, he sent Buddy over to clean it up, and the boy had just begun to pick up the litter when a Secret Service agent came over and brusquely asked him what he was doing loitering around the Carter house. "Mr. Billy sent me over to clean up this lot," he explained. "Well, you'll have to move on," the agent ordered. "Yes, sir," Buddy said, and left.

When he got home, Billy asked why he wasn't doing the job he gave him. Buddy explained and Billy said, "Why in the hell didn't you tell him who you were?"

"I just didn't want to," Buddy said. Like his daddy, he wanted to be himself, not Billy Carter's son.

After Billy left for Americus, Kim said she had to take care of a few things before the guests arrived. Marle, Billy and Sybil's fourteen-year-old daughter, had been in and out of the kitchen all morning long and heard Kim's comment. She came over without a word and extended her arms to the baby in Kim's lap. He reached up and went into Marle's embrace.

Having had four teen-agers of my own, I know about the usual reaction of adolescents to parental requests for their assistance in chores around the house. Though it may appear to be a saccharine fictionalizing of this household, during that whole day of busy preparations, I never once heard Sybil ask her children for assistance; they were constantly volunteering their help. Earl went to each of his sisters as needed, and they were obviously delighted with the job.

Marle seemed the most maternal of the girls, and the most excited teen-ager of all. She was almost beside herself as she talked about Tom T. Hall's visit. She had most of his records in her bedroom and today she was going to meet him. Forget the Beatles and the Righteous Brothers. To this 4-H Club president, country-and-western Tom T. was it! And he was coming to *her* house.

When he walked in the door about two hours later, she stared at him in mute disbelief. When he shook her hand, it was obvious that the world stood still. The band set up their instruments in the family room, and as they played their first number, Marle pressed through the group and whispered in my ear, "Aunt Ruth, have him play 'I Love.'" The next number was her request and her day was climbing close to ecstasy.

It was a marvelous party. Guests began to arrive about eleven o'clock, and the family and their friends mingled moments of eating Sybil's ample spread of baked ham, roast turkey, fried chicken casserole, several kinds of salad and hors d'oeuvres, homemade ice cream and pecan pie with Tom T.'s informal concert until four o'clock that afternoon.

I left early in the evening to visit Mother at the Pond House, and the next day I returned to talk more with Sybil. I wanted to compare her feelings about her children with my own observations. I was especially interested in little Mandy, her nine-year-old daughter.

"Sybil," I said, "there's something very different about Mandy, isn't there?" I had watched this child with the Dresden doll face and intense, big blue eyes as Kim, Sybil, and I were seated around the kitchen table on the night before the party. She said only a few words the whole evening. But I caught her staring at me several times. I diverted my eyes so I wouldn't embarrass her. Her gaze was so intense. It was as though she was trying to know my very soul.

"Yes," Sybil replied, "Mandy is the most sensitive of the children. I remember once when we were eating she began to cry. And when I asked her what was wrong she said, 'Momma, I don't want all those children who don't have anything to eat tonight to go hungry.' Well, that was strange for a seven-year-old to say when no one had been talking about it. Somewhere, maybe on TV, she had heard about starving children and it kept on haunting her."

Inscrutable Mandy. She clings and demands more patience to be around, but not because she is pampered or spoiled. It is, it seems, because she has an adult concern for life in a child's heart.

The emotional opposite to Mandy is their eighteen-year-old daughter, Jana Kae. She is a distaff version of Billy, all perpetual motion, independence, don't-fence-me-in. On the day of the party she was rarely in the house for more than an hour. She was driving here and there to who-knows-where? God made her lovely face and her natural platinum blond hair formal. The rest of her trim form she has made tomboy casual. She is rarely in anything but a T-shirt and a pair of well-worn faded Levi's. After graduating from high school, Jana Kae informed her parents that she didn't want to go on to college; she wanted to become a game warden. Billy accepted her decision and encouraged her to apply for the position. She is in her apprenticeship now.

Throughout the whole, hectic, happy day of the party, the star performance wasn't given by T. T. Hall, in Billy's estimation. The baby was his headliner. He would gravitate to little Earl every few minutes. He never held him long. He just picked him up, talked to him, or bounced him on his knee, and then after a few minutes he passed him over to one of the children or took him back to his bedroom to lay him down. Without a doubt one of the mooring lines that has kept Billy from flying off into space through the recent months of pressure is his attachment to the baby.

Sybil once said to me, "There's something about Billy that when people are around him it makes them feel better about things." That is just what I was feeling. As I prepared to go home I knew I was loved by this man. Somehow his devotion to his children had infected my spirit, too. To this day, he may take business or rare pleasure trips, but he never spends a minute on the road he doesn't have to. If it takes all night, he will fly or drive to be home with his wife and children.

I was in Plains just one month after Jimmy's inauguration. By then Billy was more than a celebrity; he had become a sort of folk hero. I was standing in the peanut warehouse office with Sybil when he came rushing in to say good-bye. He was leaving on a three o'clock flight for New York City to be interviewed by Tom Snyder on his "Tomorrow Show." Dragging on his cigarette and grinning, he said, "Sybil, do I look okay?" He had on a new Ultrasuede rust-colored leisure suit.

"Oh, Billy, you just look great," Sybil said, "but your coat lining shows a little."

Billy picked up a pair of scissors which were standing in a pencil holder and handed them to Sybil. Backing up to her he said, "I'm in a hurry. Cut it out fast."

"Billy, I'm not cutting this lining out of your new suit," she protested. "You must be crazy."

"But what difference does it make, Sybil? I'll only be gone a few hours and I'm not taking my coat off."

Billy couldn't wait for her to tear out and resew his sagging lining and it would have been wrong to cut it out. So Sybil found a strip of superstick tape and presto, the job was done.

As Billy walked out, his parting words were, "Sybil, I'll be home tonight."

"Billy! How can you possibly get home tonight?"

"I'll find a way!" he said.

"Remember, Billy," Sybil called after him, "when you get on that show tonight, don't stick out your tongue when you take a drag off your cigarette. You know that if you do I'll get at least ten thousand letters next week from people telling me you have emphysema."

Over the roar of his car's engine, Billy shouted, "I won't, Sybil. This time I promise I won't. See you tonight." And he was off for the Big Apple. But true to his word, he arrived back home at 3:30 A.M.

During the interview, Tom Snyder had asked Billy about his plans while in New York. "What are you going to do after the show?" he said.

"I'm going home," Billy replied.

"You mean tonight?"

"Yes."

"Why do you want to do that?"

"Because I want to be with my wife and six kids."

That didn't fit the popular image of Billy Carter, redneck swinger, but he had let his guard down for a moment and the real Billy Carter stood up.

He found a flight out of La Guardia into Atlanta that night. There was no connecting flight to Albany, so he rented a car and drove the last 150 miles. It was 3:30 A.M., but he was home.

16

No Business Like Show Business

In the first year of Jimmy's presidency Billy became big business—show business. He saw it coming and had very mixed feelings about it.

During the inaugural celebration, Billy and I sat together late one evening in my room at the Washington Hilton. In a suite nearby, family and friends were in the midst of a party, but that night Billy wasn't in a festive mood. He wanted to be alone for a while and just talk. He had reclined on the sofa, kicked off his shoes, and propped his stocking feet on the coffee table. "Ruth," he said to me, "I've really created a monster"—repeating the apprehensive comment he had earlier made in an interview with Dan Rather—"and I don't know what to do with it."

With Jimmy in the White House, Billy's clowning and candor had generated a lot of public criticism but even more popular acclaim. He found himself carried along by a wave of celebrity over which he had no control. He was riding it like a champion surfer, but he soon began to wonder how much longer he could stay on top.

On one of my visits to Plains during the presidential campaign, I got a glimpse of how impossible the situation was becoming for Billy. I drove to the warehouse to say hello to him, and during the half hour I was there eight calls were received making some sort of request for a public appearance or a product endorsement. When I expressed my shock, Billy laughed. "Hell," he said, "you haven't heard nothing. One guy called the other day and said he was starting a Billy Carter Foundation. Another wanted to make Billy Carter candy bars."

Our conversation was interrupted at that moment by a man and his wife, tourists from Albuquerque, New Mexico, who walked into the warehouse and wanted Billy's autograph. "Gosh, we hate to barge in like this," said the bald, smiling stranger, "but Carol and I came all the way to Georgia just hoping we could meet you and get your autograph."

Smiling, Billy stood up, shook the man's hand, and said, "Well, good."

Carol, obviously very nervous, silently handed Billy a pen and paper on which he automatically scrawled his name. "Thank you," the man said as the two retreated toward the door. "This just makes our trip."

"Glad to see you," Billy said.

Autograph hunters and tourists were just part of his problem. Now that Jimmy was President, Billy was receiving dozens of requests every day to appear at public and private functions. Which invitations should he accept, which should he refuse? Should he charge a fee? If so, how much? These were only a few of the questions that were plaguing him.

"It sounds like you need a manager," I said.

My suggestion confirmed a thought he had had on the back burner for some time. He hated the idea of being managed, of commercializing himself, but the pressures of being the President's un-cola, refreshingly different brother weren't going to go away. He often said when asked for his autograph that "My signature isn't worth a nickel, except on a five-cent check," but the hustlers knew it could be sold for a lot more than that. One enterprising opportunist acquired beer cans Billy had signed as a favor for tourists and scalped them for five to ten dollars apiece. Nothing short of death or exile to some island would stop the constant harassment by well-meaning tourists, celebrity hounds, and the profiteers who tried to peddle his popular flesh without offering Billy a penny for his services.

So Billy decided to look for a manager. The name most often suggested was Tandy Rice, the Nashville agent who has such country-and-western stars as Kitty Wells and Tom T. Hall. One phone call to Rice's office set the wheels in motion. Tandy knew that Billy would be one of the hottest items on the celebrity circuit and wasted no time returning the call. Two days later he caught a plane for Atlanta, rented a car, and drove to Americus where he met Billy at the Best Western motel.

Tandy is a dark-haired, rather dapper, youngish-looking man who brims with a quiet self-confidence. Billy liked him immediately. Over lunch in the restaurant at the motel, Tandy got straight to the point. If Billy went with him, he said, his office would handle all requests. Tandy would require a certified check from any group or individual who booked Billy's services in advance of his appearance. Billy would retain the right to refuse any invitation before final booking was made. All travel, lodging, and security details would be handled by Tandy's staff. As Billy's agent, he would receive a percentage. It all sounded fine to Billy, but he surprised Tandy by upping the agent's take. A friend later asked him why he didn't stick with the first price. "Because he's looking after my interests," Billy answered, "and I want him to know I appreciate it."

Two weeks after Billy signed on with Tandy, he and Sybil were invited to fly up to Tandy's establishment in Nashville. Tom T. Hall was giving a concert at the Grand Ole Opry, the

Vatican of country-and-western music. Tandy knew that Tom
T. was a favorite of theirs and he thought this would be a good
time to acquaint them with his office and staff while showing
them a mixture of greasepaint and the talented folk singing
which he so skillfully marketed.

On the first night of their visit, Billy and Sybil attended Tom
T.'s concert, and when they arrived at the music hall they were
ushered down to the front row. It was a thrilling experience for
Sybil. She really has no interest in Billy's celebrity status, and
she finds the sudden fame and notoriety disconcerting because
it is devoid of the two qualities she has and appreciates in
others: emotional warmth and reality. But here she felt a closeness. The people they had met during the day seemed sincerely
happy to see them. They were like a family, and as they walked
down the aisle to their seats, people called out, "Hi there,
Billy," "Glad to see you here, Mrs. Carter," "We're sure glad
you came to Nashville." By now Sybil was glad, too, very glad.

Tom T.'s throat was gimpy that night. Someone trying to be
helpful had recommended he gargle with brandy. It soothed
both his throat and his brain. He knew his performance was less
than his best. He is a pro and he gave his audience the best he
had. But that best was a bit rusty and Tom T. kept forgetting
the words to the songs he himself had written. Suddenly someone in the crowd called out, "Tom T., get Sybil up there to help
you." Tom T. didn't even know that Sybil could carry a tune,
but desperately he called out, "Sybil, won't you join me?"

He was singing one of Sybil's favorites, "Watermelon Wine."
She and her children had played his record of it so often that
she knew it, as well as most of his other songs, by heart. Even
so she would have refused to go up on the stage under ordinary
circumstances. But she knew Tom T. was having some difficulty and that motivated her enough to ignore her pounding
heart and flushed face and walk up on the stage beside Tom T.

at the microphone. The audience applauded loudly. No doubt part of their enthusiasm was the realization that she was being a good sport. Everyone knew she was Billy's wife and they were ready to like her for that reason alone. But after she finished the first few bars of the song, they knew they were being treated to genuine beauty.

When her strong, lilting soprano voice faded out on the last note of the song, the people were on their feet cheering and clapping. Tom T., the showman, had pulled this one out—with a little help from a friend. "Sybil," Billy said as they left the concert that night, "you were sure great." At last, Sybil let out a big sigh. Her world was round again.

After Billy hit the celebrity circuit under Tandy's management, he discovered that he was being paid to do the thing he had always enjoyed most—talk in his funny, profane, and irreverent way about politics, religion, or whatever else the subject might happen to be. He also found out that being funny when you have to isn't much fun. But he still loved talking about his favorite subjects. Billy has views on every policy and every issue, and he often verbalized what the average man felt but had no platform from which to speak. When questioned about Washington bureaucrats, for instance, Billy came down hard on them, especially the Occupational Safety and Health Administration. Its stupid, irrelevant, and unnecessary regulations, he said, sometimes put small businesses *out* of business. "When they sent their inspector to my warehouse," Billy remarked, "he didn't know the peanut shelter from the cotton gin. He took some pictures of beer boxes out front and it cost me 20 percent of the cost of my whole plant just to meet their air pollution regulations." He also enjoyed knocking the IRS and constantly threatened to take them to court. Then he would laugh and say, "I know I can't, but I like to keep them scared."

When accused of being an opportunist and cashing in on Jimmy's fame, Billy would only laugh and say, "If people are crazy enough to pay me to speak, I'm crazy enough to do it." But he insists he and his family haven't changed. "I always did like good food, good liquor, good beer, and good automobiles. I had them before and I have them now—no more, no less." All Billy's family still work except for the two small ones. Sybil, now that she no longer keeps the books in the peanut warehouse, is keeping Billy's books. Marle works at the drugstore two days a week; Jana is a park ranger; Buddy works at the filling station; and Kim had to be forced to quit her part-time job at college when her life became so busy nearing graduation.

Billy found that the celebrity circuit was usually pretty hard work, but once he had committed himself to a job, he did it— and did it well. He made it clear, however, that he would not take part in any political activities. Yet people sometimes tried to put him in that position. One time both Billy and I were scheduled to appear at a gathering that was labeled a benefit. I accepted because Billy and I had never appeared together and I thought it would be great fun. We entered the meeting hall together. A band was playing and everything was draped in red, white, and blue streamers. Billy stopped abruptly and his face turned red. "It's a political function," he said. "Let's go. We are not staying."

I understood what he meant. More than once I had been invited to do my work only to find out upon arrival that there were other motives involved on the part of the sponsors—and not always good motives.

There were many changes in Billy's life after Jimmy became President, perhaps one of the more dramatic being his decision to resign as the managing partner of the successful Carter peanut business in Plains. With all the tourists in town, it was virtually impossible for him to conduct the business. His customers, who were also his friends, simply did not want to come into the warehouse. But aside from that, Billy had two main reasons for giving up the business: One, his desire to spend more time with his family, and two, the demands of speaking and making appearances on the celebrity circuit. He still owned a 15 percent interest in the business when he stepped down, of course, and he owned outright his popular service station, plus some 173 acres in Sumter County. Billy had proved himself to be a good businessman in many ways, but I discovered when he first started out on the speaking circuit that he had often been too generous in helping his friends. He thought nothing of signing bank notes for almost anyone, often people who took advantage of his good heart, and he found himself on numerous occasions paying off other people's debts. He did it without complaint, but a good portion of the money from his early public appearances went to pay off such loans.

There were plenty of groups willing to pay Billy's going rate, five thousand dollars per public appearance. He noted once that he did not solicit any of the appearances, and only accepted one out of every twenty invitations. "I disappoint a lot of people if I don't come," he said. And he genuinely enjoyed a lot of his appearances, especially the give-and-take with people from all over the country. He was fielding questions in Oakland, California, one day when someone asked him for his definition of a redneck. "I really ain't sure what a redneck is," Billy responded, "even though I was born one. But I guess he's the brother that didn't get elected."

Billy also enjoyed doing charitable work, occasionally, without any fee at all, a tendency which drove his agent up the wall. Yet there were frustrations, too. The travel schedule was so hectic that it became a strain on Billy's marriage and the rest of his family. Sybil loves Billy, I think, as much as any wife could ever love a husband, but she hated it when he was gone for days at a time. Nor did she like to travel and make public appearances with him. When they did appear together, delighted audiences found that Sybil's charm and gentle wit were more than a match for Billy's brand of humor. But she didn't enjoy being in the spotlight the way Billy did. Even when she went along, Billy was so much the center of attention that the crowds failed to see that she was there, too. They were all over Billy, but when introduced to Sybil, there was just a brief glance and a quick hello, and then back to Billy. It was almost as if she didn't exist.

The tension in their marriage got very difficult toward the end of 1977, and at one point my husband spent a fair amount of time talking with Sybil. He told her it was a difficult thing at best being married to a Carter because of the fierce independence and the variety of interests most of us have. I can testify that he was speaking from his own experience, and I have always valued the kind of support he has given me. I think his talking to Sybil helped a good deal, and Billy has worked since then at spending more time with his family. For him nothing can take the place of Sybil and the children.

It was perhaps inevitable that Billy's name would come to be associated with beer. Ever since he had opened up his Amoco station, beer had been his trademark. The idea to capitalize on that association came from the Fall City Brewing Company— why not market a Billy beer? Billy was agreeable. Thirteen special brews were prepared and Billy went to Louisville for the tasting treat. Blindfolded, he was asked to make a first, a second, and a third choice. The ritual was repeated the next day, and from the thirteen brews, Billy again chose the three best. The ritual was repeated for a third time, and the owners were amazed to discover that Billy's first choice had been the same each day. So that was the special brew that became Billy Beer.

Billy later told me that when the beer was put on the market, its projected sales for the first year were attained in thirty days. People expected it to be a joke, but Billy Beer turned out to be a pleasing taste. Billy had once again proved himself to be a shrewd businessman.

His public appearances on behalf of Billy Beer and for a variety of other occasions made for a hectic schedule. In the spring of 1978, Billy was away from home on a tour and woke up in the middle of the night to go to the bathroom. He caught one foot in the bedspread and fell, banging his head severely. Billy being Billy, he saw no reason to call a doctor or go to the hospital. Fortunately, there was a doctor, a plastic surgeon, at his first appearance the next day who expressed concern about the gash on Billy's forehead. Billy refused to let the doctor stitch up the wound, but he did let him clean and bandage it. And Billy promised after that weekend of appearances that he would check into the hospital back home in Sumter County. He kept his promise, and a doctor friend, who had been trying to get him to check into the hospital for a routine physical in any case, took advantage of it. He kept Billy in the hospital long enough to run every conceivable kind of test. Happily, all the tests showed Billy to be in excellent health.

Busy as he was, he was never too busy to grant a special request. A high school graduation class wrote Billy to invite him to give the commencement address in May 1978. "We have only eight people in our graduating class, and, Billy, we really want you to be the one to address us. But we don't have any money to pay you. The only thing we can promise is all the Billy Beer you can drink."

The plea of these young people hit a responsive note with Billy, and he insisted that the commencement address be inserted in his schedule. It turned out to be a special event for all concerned. Billy loved every minute of it and closed his address with a great pearl of wisdom. "And, class, remember one thing if you forget everything else. If you want to become a success in life, have your brother elected President of the United States."

I have thought a lot about Billy and why so many people are drawn to him, from the young people in a high school graduating class to a man like former Secretary of State Henry Kissinger. I often remember the question Mr. Kissinger asked me when we first met at that luncheon at the Mexican Embassy in Washington: "Would you please tell me about your brother Billy?" But there is more to that story. As it happened I sat next to Mr. Kissinger during the luncheon, and at one point I found myself talking not to Mr. Kissinger but to the man on my other side. He, too, was interested in Billy, and I said to him that I thought Billy's main philosophy of life was to find happiness in the moment. If something is good, fine. But if something turns out badly, then Billy puts it behind him and goes on to something else. "He never grieves about the past," I remember saying.

The man next to me knew Secretary Kissinger well, and he knew something I did not know: Mr. Kissinger had been extraordinarily depressed at the notion that his career as Secretary of State was coming to an end. He has, of course, since then gone on to other achievements, many of them, but at that time Mr. Kissinger apparently felt his life as well as his career were virtually over. At one point in our conversation, my luncheon companion leaned over to attract Mr. Kissinger's attention. "Henry," he said, "I want you to hear this. I want you to hear Ruth talking about her brother Billy."

I spoke again about the philosophy I thought was central to Billy's character: Never grieve about the past. I said, too, I remember, that every time I'm around Billy I find I love life more and I care more for people. I do not know if Billy's philosophy helped to change Mr. Kissinger's life. But I do know that I was amused when I heard him say later at the luncheon that he had just made up his mind what he was going to do. He had decided that he and his wife, Nancy, were going to Acapulco for a few days of rest and living in the moment and happiness and thinking about his own future plans.

I did mean what I said, though, about Billy's love of life and people, and of his ability to convey that love to others. That really is my brother Billy's genius.

Index